Exercises to Accompany

A WRITER'S REFERENCE

Second Edition

Diana Hacker

Bedford Books *of* St. Martin's Press • Boston

For information, write St. Martin's Press, Inc.
175 Fifth Avenue, New York, NY 10010

Editorial Offices: Bedford Books *of* St. Martin's Press
29 Winchester Street, Boston, MA 02116

ISBN 0–312–05253–7

A Note for Instructors

The exercise sets in this booklet are keyed to specific sections in *A Writer's Reference*. If you have adopted *A Writer's Reference* as a text, you are welcome to photocopy any or all of these exercises for a variety of possible uses:

—as homework
—as classroom practice
—as quizzes
—as individualized self-teaching assignments
—as a support for a writing center or learning lab

This exercise booklet is also available for student purchase.

The exercises are double-spaced, and the instructions ask students to edit the sentences with cross-outs and insertions, not simply to recopy them with corrections. Students will thus receive practice in the same editing techniques they are expected to apply in their own drafts.

Most exercise sets begin with an example that is done for the student, followed by five lettered sentences for which answers are provided in the back of the booklet. The sets then continue with five or ten numbered sentences whose answers are given in the instructor's answer key only. If you want students to work independently, checking all of their revisions themselves, you may of course reproduce the answer key.

A Note for Students

The exercises in this booklet are designed to accompany *A Writer's Reference*. To benefit from them, you must first read the corresponding section in the book (such as E1, Parallelism), which is illustrated with sentences similar to those in the exercises.

Most of the exercise sets consist of five lettered sentences and five or ten numbered sentences. Answers to the lettered sentences appear in the back of this booklet so that you may test your understanding without the help of an instructor. Instructors use the numbered sentences for a variety of purposes — as homework or as quizzes, for example. If your instructor prefers that you use all of the exercise sentences for self-study, he or she may provide you with an answer key to both the lettered and the numbered sentences.

All exercises are double-spaced, allowing you to edit the sentences with cross-outs and insertions instead of recopying whole sentences. *A Writer's Reference* shows you how to edit, and a sample sentence at the beginning of each exercise set demonstrates the technique. Editing is the revision technique used by nearly all practicing writers. You will find that it has three important advantages over recopying: It is much faster, it allows you to focus on the problem at hand, and it prevents you from introducing new errors as you revise.

Contents

ESL Trouble Spots

Punctuation

Mechanics

Basic Grammar

Answers to Lettered Exercises

EFFECTIVE SENTENCES

EXERCISE E1-1 Parallelism   If you have problems with this exercise, see pp. 33–34 in *A Writer's Reference*, Second Edition.

Edit the following sentences to correct faulty parallelism. Revisions of lettered sentences appear in the back of the booklet. Example:

> **We began the search by calling the Department of Social Services and**
> *requesting*
> ~~requested~~ **a list of licensed day-care centers in our area.**

a. The system has capabilities such as communicating with other computers, processing records, and mathematical functions.

b. The personnel officer told me that I would answer the phone, welcome visitors, distribute mail, and some typing.

c. This summer I want a job more than to go to Disney World.

d. Mary told the judge that she had been pulled out of a line of fast-moving traffic and of her perfect driving record.

e. Nancy not only called the post office but she checked with the neighbors to see if the package had come.

1. Many states are reducing property taxes for homeowners as well as extend financial aid in the form of tax credits to renters.

2. Arch-ups are done on the floor face down, with arms extended over the head, toes pointed, and knees stay straight.

3. The boys decided that either Carla had hidden the money or had never had it in the first place.

4. During basic training, I was not only told what to do but also what to think.

5. The Food and Drug Administration has admitted that sodium nitrite can deform the fetuses of pregnant women and it can cause serious harm to anemic persons.

6. Bill finds it harder to be fair to himself than being fair to others.

7. Mother told me either to practice the violin more regularly or stop taking lessons.

8. Your adviser familiarizes you with the school and how to select classes appropriate for your curriculum.

9. To administer the poison, the tribe's sorcerers put it in their victims' food, throw it into their huts, or it can be dropped into their mouths or nostrils while they sleep.

10. The babysitter was expected to feed two children, entertain them, take phone messages, and some cleaning in the kitchen.

EXERCISE E2-1   Needed words   If you have problems with this exercise, see pp. 34–36 in *A Writer's Reference,* Second Edition.

Add any words needed for grammatical or logical completeness in the following sentences. Revisions of lettered sentences appear in the back of the booklet. Example:

that
The officer at the desk feared⌃the prisoner in the interrogation room would escape.

a. Carmen believed all four politicians on the talk show were lying.

b. Some say that Ella Fitzgerald's renditions of Cole Porter's songs are better than any singer.

c. SETI (the Search for Extraterrestrial Intelligence) has and will continue to excite interest among space buffs.

d. Samantha got along better with the chimpanzees than Albert.

e. Myra was both interested and concerned about the contents of her father's will.

1. Their starting salaries are higher than other professionals with more seniority.

2. For many years Americans had trust and affection for Walter Cronkite.

3. We invited all the neighbors whom we knew and enjoyed football as much as we did.

4. Our nursing graduates are as skilled, if not more skilled than, those of any other state college.

5. Jupiter is larger than any planet in our solar system.

6. State officials were more concerned with the damage than what caused it.

7. Great-uncle John's car resembled other bootleggers: it had a smoke screen device useful in case of pursuit by the sheriff.

8. Thomas decided to join the army after his freshman year and been in it ever since.

9. Many citizens do not believe the leaders of this administration are serious about reducing the deficit.

10. It was obvious that the students liked the new teacher more than the principal.

Edit the following sentences to correct misplaced modifiers. Revisions of lettered sentences appear in the back of the booklet. Example:

in a telephone survey

Answering questions∧can be annoying.~~in a telephone survey.~~∧

a. He only wanted to buy three roses, not a dozen.

b. Within the next few years, orthodontists will be using the technique Kurtz developed as standard practice.

c. Celia received a flier about a workshop on making a kimono from a Japanese nun.

d. The Secret Service was falsely accused of mishandling the attempted assassination by the media.

e. Each state would set a program into motion of recycling all reusable products.

1. We hope Monica will realize that providing only for her children's material needs is harmful before it is too late.

2. The orderly confessed that he had given a lethal injection to the patient after ten hours of grilling by the police.

3. Eric took a course at the university that represents a new low in education.

4. It just took experience with two clients to convince my mother to avoid interior design.

5. He promised never to remarry at her deathbed.

EXERCISE E3-2   Dangling modifiers   If you have problems with this exercise, see pp. 38–40 in *A Writer's Reference*, Second Edition.

Edit the following sentences to correct dangling modifiers. Most sentences can be revised in more than one way. Revisions of lettered sentences appear in the back of the booklet. Example:

a student must complete

To acquire a degree in almost any field, ∧ **two science courses.** ~~must be~~

~~completed.~~

a. Reaching the heart, a bypass was performed on the severely blocked arteries.

b. Nestled in the cockpit, the pounding of the engine was muffled only slightly by my helmet.

c. Feeling unprepared for the exam, the questions were as hard as June's instructor had suggested they would be.

d. While still a beginner at tennis, the coaches recruited my sister to train for the Olympics.

e. To protest the arms buildup, bonfires were set throughout the park.

1. When flashing, do not speed through a yellow light.

2. Exhausted from battling the tide and the undertow, a welcome respite appeared in the swimmer's view — the beach!

3. As president of the missionary circle, one of Grandmother's duties is to raise money for the church.

4. Spending four hours on the operating table, a tumor as large as a golf ball was removed from the patient's stomach.

5. To become an attorney, two degrees must be earned and a bar examination must be passed.

EXERCISE E4-1 Shifts If you have problems with this exercise, see pp. 40–43 in *A Writer's Reference*, Second Edition.

Edit the following sentences to eliminate distracting shifts. Revisions of lettered sentences appear in the back of the booklet. Example:

> For most people it is not easy to quit smoking once ~~you~~ are hooked.
>
> *they* (inserted above "you")

a. We waited in the emergency room for about an hour. Finally, the nurse comes in and tells us that we are in the wrong place.

b. Newspapers put the lurid details of an armed robbery on page 1, and the warm, human-interest stories are relegated to page G-10.

c. A minister often has a hard time because they have to please so many different people.

d. We drove for eight hours until we reached the South Dakota Badlands. You could hardly believe the eeriness of the landscape at dusk.

e. The question is whether ferrets bred in captivity have the instinct to prey on prairie dogs or is this a learned skill.

1. Police officers always follow strict codes of safety. For example, always point the barrel of the gun upward when the gun is not in use.

2. For a minimal fee one may join the class. Once you arrive for class, a medical form is filled out of by each person and submitted to the instructor.

3. According to Dr. Winfield, a person who wants to become a doctor must first earn a B.S. degree. After this they must take a medical aptitude test called the MCAT.

4. The principal asked whether I had seen the fight and, if so, why didn't I report it.

5. A single parent often has only their ingenuity to rely on.

6. When the director travels, you will make the hotel and airline reservations and you will arrange for a rental car. A detailed itinerary must also be prepared.

7. As I was pulling in the decoys, you could see and hear the geese heading back to the bay.

8. Rescue workers put water on her face and lifted her head gently onto a pillow. Finally, she opens her eyes.

9. With a little self-discipline and a desire to improve oneself, you too can enjoy the benefits of running.

10. We always follow a strict routine at the campground. First we erected the tent, rolled out the sleeping bags, and set up the kitchen; then we all head for the swimming pool.

EXERCISE E5-1 Mixed constructions If you have problems with this exercise, see pp. 43–45 in *A Writer's Reference*, Second Edition.

Edit the following sentences to untangle mixed constructions. Revisions of lettered sentences appear in the back of the booklet. Example:

  L
~~By~~ ̸loosening the soil around your jade plant will help the air and nutrients penetrate to the roots.

a. My instant reaction was filled with anger and disappointment.

b. I brought a problem into the house that my mother wasn't sure how to handle it.

---

c. It is through the misery of others that has made old Harvey rich.

d. A cloverleaf is when traffic on limited-access freeways can change direction.

e. Bowman established the format in which future football card companies would emulate for years to come.

1. The more experienced pilots in the system Zeke assigned two aircraft to them.

2. Depending on the number and strength of drinks, the amount of time that has passed since the last drink, and one's body weight determines the concentration of alcohol in the blood.

3. The decline in the rate of live births in the country was decreasing.

4. By pushing the button for the insert mode opens the computer's memory.

5. The reason the Eskimos were forced to eat their dogs was because the caribou, on which they depended for food, migrated out of reach.

6. To look at rolling hills of virgin snow or snow-capped evergreens is far more beautiful than the brown slush on city streets.

7. Pat had to train herself on a mainframe computer that was designed for data entry but it was not intended for word processing.

8. One service available to military personnel living on base, the Special Services Building, provides half-price tickets to local movie theaters.

9. In the section of the perimeter for which my unit was responsible came under fire.

10. The little time we have together we try to use it wisely.

EXERCISE E6-1 **Coordination and subordination** If you
have problems with this exercise, see pp. 45–49 in *A Writer's
Reference*, Second Edition.

In the following paragraphs, combine choppy sentences by subordinating minor
ideas or by coordinating ideas of equal importance. More than one effective revision
is possible.

Some scientists favor continued research to advance the technology of genetic

engineering. They argue that they are only refining the process of selective breeding

that has benefited society for many years. For centuries, they claim, scientists have

recognized variations in plant and animal species from generation to generation. In

the early nineteenth century, scientists explained those variations as part of an

evolutionary process. They called this process natural selection. Later scientists

found ways to duplicate this process of natural selection. They did not want to leave

the process to chance. They developed the technique of selective breeding.

Dairy farmers use selective breeding. They do it to increase production from

their herds. They choose the best milk-producing cows for breeding. These cows

have certain genetic traits. These traits make them top producers. Breeding them

selectively increases the chance that the offspring will inherit those same genetic

traits. Then they will be top producers too. For the same reasons, farmers identify

the cows that are low producers. They choose not to use them for breeding.

Scientists argue that genetic engineering is not much different from selective

breeding. They claim that it can produce similar positive results. Society, they say,

should support their research. Society can only benefit, as it has in the past.

EXERCISE E6-2   Coordination and subordination   If you
have problems with this exercise, see pp. 45–49 in *A Writer's
Reference*, Second Edition.

Combine or restructure the following sentences by subordinating minor ideas or by
coordinating ideas of equal importance. You must decide which ideas are minor because the sentences are given out of context. Revisions of lettered sentences appear
in the back of the booklet. Example:

> **The team rowed until their strength nearly gave out and finally**
> *where they*   *to celebrate*
> **returned to shore,~~and~~ had a party on the beach ~~and celebrated~~ the**
>   ∧   ∧
> **start of the season.**

a. A couple of minutes went by, and the teacher walked in smiling.

b. The losing team was made up of superstars. These superstars acted as

    isolated individuals on the court.

c. We keep our use of insecticides, herbicides, and fungicides to a minimum.

    We are concerned about the environment.

d. The aides help the younger children with reading and math. These are the

    children's weakest subjects.

e. My first sky dive was from an altitude of 12,500 feet, and it was the most

    frightening experience of my life.

1. The American crocodile could once be found in abundance in southern

    Florida. It is now being threatened with extinction.

2. I noticed that the sky was glowing orange and red. I bent down to crawl into

    the bunker.

3. Sister Consilio was enveloped in a black robe with only her face and hands

    visible. She was an imposing figure.

4. Cocaine is an addictive drug and it can seriously harm you both physically and mentally, if death doesn't get you first.

5. We met every Monday morning in the home of one of the members. These meetings would last about three hours.

6. Marta was her father's favorite. She felt free to do whatever she wanted.

7. He walked up to the pitcher's mound. He dug his toe into the ground. He swung his arm around backward and forward. Then he threw the ball and struck the batter out.

8. Alan walked over to his car, and he noticed a few unusual dark spots on the hood.

9. The lift chairs were going around very fast. They were bumping the skiers into their seats.

10. The first football card set was released by the Goudey Gum Company in 1933. The set featured only three football players. They were Red Grange, Bronko Nagurski, and Knute Rockne.

EXERCISE E6-3   Faulty subordination   If you have problems with this exercise, see pp. 48–49 in *A Writer's Reference*, Second Edition.

In each of the following sentences, the idea that the writer wished to emphasize is buried in a subordinate construction. Restructure each sentence so that the independent clause expresses the major idea and lesser ideas are subordinated. Revisions of lettered sentences appear in the back of the booklet. Example:

Though
∧ **Catherine has weathered many hardships, ~~though~~ she has rarely become discouraged.** [*Emphasize that Catherine has rarely become discouraged.*]

a. Our team finally acquired an expert backstroker, who enabled us to win every relay for the rest of the season. [*Emphasize the wins, not acquiring the backstroker.*]

b. The senator was planning a trip to Spain and Portugal when the travel agent canceled the trip because of terrorist activities. [*Emphasize the cancellation.*]

c. I presented the idea of job sharing to my supervisors, who to my surprise were delighted with the idea. [*Emphasize the supervisors' response to the idea.*]

d. Although native Hawaiians try to preserve their ancestors' sacred customs, outsiders have forced changes on them. [*Emphasize the Hawaiians' attempt to preserve their customs.*]

e. Sharon's country kitchen, which overlooks a field where horses and cattle graze among old tombstones, was formerly a lean-to porch. [*Emphasize that the kitchen overlooks the field.*]

1. My grandfather, who raised his daughters the old-fashioned way, was born eighty-six years ago in Puerto Rico. [*Emphasize how the grandfather raised his daughters.*]

2. The building housed a school, a grocery store, an auto repair shop, and two families when it burned to the ground last week. [*Emphasize that the building burned down.*]

3. Louis's team worked with the foreign mission by building new churches and restoring those damaged by hurricanes. [*Emphasize the building and restoring.*]

4. We were traveling down I-94 when we were hit in the rear by a speeding Oldsmobile. [*Emphasize the accident.*]

5. Although Sarah felt that we lacked decent transportation, our family owned a Jeep, a pickup truck, and a sports car. [*Emphasize Sarah's feeling that the family lacked decent transportation.*]

EXERCISE E7-1   Sentence variety   If you have problems with this exercise, see pp. 49–50 in *A Writer's Reference*, Second Edition.

Edit the following paragraph to increase variety in sentence structure.

I have spent thirty years of my life on a tobacco farm, and I cannot understand why people smoke. The whole process of raising tobacco involves deadly chemicals. The ground is treated for mold and chemically fertilized before the tobacco seed is ever planted. The seed is planted and begins to grow, and then the bed is treated with weed killer. The plant is then transferred to the field. It is sprayed with poison to kill worms about two months later. Then the time for harvest approaches, and the plant is sprayed once more with a chemical to retard the growth of suckers. The tobacco is harvested and hung in a barn to dry. These barns are havens for birds. The birds defecate all over the leaves. After drying, these leaves are divided by color, and no feces are removed. They are then sold to the tobacco companies. I do not know what the tobacco companies do after they receive the tobacco. I do not need to know. They cannot remove what I know is in the leaf and on the leaf. I don't want any of it to pass through my mouth.

WORD CHOICE

Edit the following sentences for problems in usage. If a sentence is correct, write "correct" after it. Answers to lettered sentences appear in the back of the booklet. Example:

                                               an
   The pediatrician gave my daughter ~~a~~ injection for her allergy.

a. The amount of horses a Comanche warrior had in his possession indicated the wealth of his family.

b. The cat just set there watching his prey.

c. We will contact you by phone as soon as the tickets arrive.

d. Changing attitudes toward alcohol have effected the beer industry.

e. Chris redesigned the boundary plantings to try and improve the garden's overall design.

1. When he learned that I had seven children, four of which were still at home, Gill smiled and said that he loved children.

2. Everyone in our office is enthused about this project.

3. Please phone for an hotel reservation at the Brown Palace in Denver.

4. Gary decided to loan his cousin money for a year's tuition.

5. These are the kind of problems that can take months to correct.

6. Most sleds are pulled by no less than two dogs and no more than ten.

7. I usually shop first at the French Market, which is further away, and then stop at Food Mart on my way home.

8. The Japanese bather could care less whether you use your washcloth as a fig leaf.

9. Alan had been lying on the sidewalk unconscious for nearly two hours before help arrived.

10. This afternoon I plan to lay out in the sun and begin working on a tan.

EXERCISE W2-1   Wordy sentences   If you have problems with this exercise, see pp. 66–69 in *A Writer's Reference*, Second Edition.

Edit the following sentences for wordiness. Revisions of lettered sentences appear in the back of the booklet. Example:

The Wilsons moved into the house ~~in spite of the fact that~~ *even though* the back door was only ten yards from the train tracks.

a. When visitors come to visit her, Grandmother just stares at the wall.

b. Dr. Sandford has seen problems like yours countless numbers of times.

c. In my opinion, Bloom's race for the governorship is a futile exercise.

d. If there are any new fares, then they must be reported by message to all of our transportation offices.

e. In Biology 10A you will be assigned a faculty tutor who will be available to assign you eight taped modules and help you clarify any information on the tapes.

1. Seeing the barrels, the driver immediately slammed on his brakes.

2. The thing data sets are used for is communicating with other computers.

3. The town of New Harmony, located in Indiana, was founded as a utopian community.

4. In the early eighties, some analysts viewed Soviet expansion as an effort to achieve nothing less than world dominance, if not outright control of the world.

5. You will be the contact person for arranging interviews between the institute and the office of personnel.

6. Martin Luther King, Jr., was a man who set a high standard for future leaders to meet.

7. Your job will be the transportation of luggage from the carts to the conveyor belts.

8. A typical autocross course consists of at least two straightaways, and the rest of the course is made up of numerous slaloms and several sharp turns.

9. The program is called the Weight Control Program, and it has been remarkably successful in helping airmen and airwomen lose weight.

10. The price of driving while drunk or while intoxicated can be extremely high.

EXERCISE W2-2 Wordy sentences If you have problems with this exercise, see pp. 66–69 in *A Writer's Reference*, Second Edition.

Edit the following paragraph for wordiness.

We examined the old house from top to bottom. In fact, we started in the attic, which was hot and dusty, and made our way down two flights of stairs, and down one more descent, which was a spiral staircase, into the basement. On our way back up, we thought we heard the eerie noise, the one that had startled us from our

---

sound sleep in the first place. This time the noise was at the top of the staircase
that led to the second-floor hallway. We froze and stood quietly at exactly the same
moment, listening very intently. Finally, after a few moments, someone said, "Why
don't we all go in together and see what it is?" Cautiously, with great care, we
stepped over the threshold into the dark hallway, which disappeared into darkness
in front of us. There was an unearthly emanating light shining from underneath the
door that led into the kitchen. All at once we jumped when we heard a loud crashing
sound from behind that door. Before we could rush into the kitchen at high speed,
the light went out suddenly, and instantly we were in total pitch black darkness. I
thought I heard someone's teeth chattering; then I realized with a shock that it was
my own teeth I heard chattering. Without saying a word, we backed silently away
from the kitchen door — no one wanted to go in now. Then it was as if someone had
shot off a gun, because before we realized what we were doing, we tore up the stairs
as fast as we could, and we dove into our beds and pulled the covers up and over us
to shut out any more frightening sounds and thoughts.

EXERCISE W3-1   Jargon and pretentious language   If you
have problems with this exercise, see pp. 70–71 in *A Writer's
Reference*, Second Edition.

Edit the following sentences to eliminate jargon, pretentious or flowery language,
and euphemisms. You may need to make substantial changes in some sentences. Revisions of lettered sentences appear in the back of the booklet. Example:

> After two weeks in the legal department, Sue has ~~worked into~~ the
> ~~routine~~*of the office,* and her ~~functional and self-management skills~~
> ~~have~~ exceeded all expectations.
>
> *mastered* ^
> *office* ^
> *Performance has* ^

a. It is a widespread but unproven hypothesis that the parameters of significant personal change for persons in midlife are extremely narrow.

b. Have you ever been accused of flagellating a deceased equine?

c. Utilizing my elbows, I was able to crawl about ten yards to the trench.

d. When our father was selected out from his high-paying factory job, we learned what it was like to be economically depressed.

e. In the event that the recipient of the computer is unable to complete the installation, guidance may be obtained by getting in touch with the firm's main office by using its 800 telephone number.

1. Sam's arguments failed to impact positively on his parents or his male siblings.

2. As I approached the edifice of confinement where my brother was incarcerated, several inmates loudly vocalized a number of lewd remarks.

3. The nurse announced that there had been a negative patient-care outcome due to a therapeutic misadventure on the part of the surgeon.

4. When we returned from our evening perambulation, we shrank back in horror as we surmised that our domestic dwelling was being swallowed up in hellish flames.

5. The bottom line is that the company is experiencing a negative cash flow.

EXERCISE W3-2 Slang and level of formality If you have problems with this exercise, see pp. 71–73 in *A Writer's Reference*, Second Edition.

Edit the following paragraph to eliminate slang and maintain a consistent level of formality.

The graduation speaker really blew it. He should have discussed the options and challenges facing the graduating class. Instead, he shot his mouth off at us and trashed us for being lazy and pampered. He did make some good points, however. Our profs have certainly babied us by not holding fast to deadlines, by dismissing assignments that the class ragged them about, by ignoring our tardiness, and by handing out easy C's like hotcakes. Still, we resented this speech as the final word from the college establishment. It should have been the orientation speech for us when we entered as freshmen.

EXERCISE W3-3 Sexist language If you have problems with this exercise, see pp. 73–75 in *A Writer's Reference*, Second Edition.

Edit the following sentences to eliminate sexist language or sexist assumptions. Revisions of lettered sentences appear in the back of the booklet. Example:

Scholarship athletes
~~A scholarship athlete~~ must be as concerned about ~~his~~ their academic
performance as ~~he is~~ they are about ~~his~~ their athletic performance.

a. Ms. Harriet Glover, who is a doctor's wife, is the defense attorney appointed by the court. Al Jones has been assigned to work with her on the case.

b. If a young graduate is careful about investments, he can accumulate a significant sum in a relatively short period.

c. An elementary school teacher should understand the concept of nurturing if she intends to be a success.

d. Because Dr. Brown and Dr. Dorothy Coombs were the senior professors in the department, they served as co-chairmen of the promotion committee.

e. If man does not stop polluting his environment, mankind will perish.

1. I have been trained to doubt an automobile mechanic, even if he has an excellent reputation.

2. When a professor enters the lecture hall, he expects the students to be ready for class to begin.

3. Dr. Elizabeth Moore, a mother of three and a judge's wife, will be the next dean of the medical school.

4. In my hometown, the lady mayor had led the fight for a fair share of federal funds for new schools.

5. As partners in a successful real estate firm, John Crockett and Sarah Cooke have been an effective sales team. He is particularly skillful at arranging attractive mortgage packages; she is a vivacious blonde who stays fit by doing aerobics daily.

EXERCISE W4-1   Active verbs   If you have problems with this exercise, see pp. 76–77 in *A Writer's Reference*, Second Edition.

The verbs in the following sentences are italicized. Revise passive or linking verbs with active alternatives; do not change active verbs. If a sentence's verbs are all active, write the word "active" after the sentence. Revisions of lettered sentences appear in the back of the booklet. Example:

> The ranger doused the campfire before giving us
> ~~The campfire *was doused* by the ranger before we *were given*~~ a ticket
> ^
> for unauthorized use of a campsite.

a. The developing, fixing, washing, and drying of the film *are* automatically *performed* by the processor.

b. The entire operation *is overlooked* by the producer.

c. Finally the chute *caught* air and *popped* open with a jolt at around 2,000 feet.

d. Escaping into the world of drugs, I *was* rebellious about anything and everything laid down by the establishment.

e. There *were* fighting players on both sides of the rink.

1. The maintaining of an accurate and orderly log by the radiologist *is required* according to hospital protocol.

2. Sam *was* unsuccessful in his attempt to pass the first performance test.

3. In a rage, one steroid abuser *smashed* his refrigerator with a baseball bat.

4. C.B.'s *are used* to find parts, equipment, food, lodging, and anything else a trucker might need.

5. At the crack of rocket and mortar blasts, I *jumped* from the top bunk and *landed* on my buddy below, who *was crawling* on the floor looking for his boots.

6. That summer in New Hampshire, a horse *was given* to me by my grandparents.

7. The bomb bay doors *rumbled* open, and freezing air *whipped* through the plane.

8. There *were* exploding firecrackers all around us.

9. Marie *was encouraged* by her favorite biology professor to become a doctor.

10. The scholarship *will be* beneficial to part-time students only.

EXERCISE W4-2 Misused words If you have problems with this exercise, see p. 77 in *A Writer's Reference*, Second Edition.

Edit the following sentences to correct misused words. Revisions of lettered sentences appear in the back of the booklet. Example:

> *all-absorbing.*
> **The training required for a ballet dancer is ~~all-absorbent.~~**
> $\land$

a. Many of us are not persistence enough to make a change for the better.

b. Mrs. Altman's comments were meant to invoke a response from the class.

c. Sam Brown began his career as a lawyer, but now he is a real estate mongrel.

d. When Robert Frost died at age eighty-eight, he left a legacy of poems that will make him immortal for years to come.

e. This patient is kept in isolation to prevent her from obtaining our germs.

1. In 1776, the United States acclaimed its independence from England.

2. Trifle, a popular English dessert, contains a ménage of ingredients that do not always appeal to American tastes.

3. Washington's National Airport is surrounded on three sides by water.

4. Frequently I cannot do my work because the music blaring from my son's room detracts me.

5. Tom Jones is an illegal child who grows up under the care of Squire Western.

Edit the following sentences to eliminate errors in the use of idiomatic expressions.
If a sentence is correct, write "correct" after it. Answers to lettered sentences appear in the back of the booklet. Example:

We agreed to abide ~~with~~ the decision of the judge.

(*by* inserted above "with")

a. I was so angry at the salesperson that I took her bag of samples and emptied
    it on the floor in front of her.

b. Prior to the Russians' launching of *Sputnik*, *nik* was not an English suffix.

c. Try and come up with the rough outline, and we will find someone who can
    fill in the details.

d. "Your prejudice is no different than mine," she shouted.

e. The parade moved off of the street and onto the beach.

1. Be sure and report on the danger of releasing genetically engineered
    bacteria into the atmosphere.

2. Why do you assume that embezzling bank assets is so different than robbing
    the bank?

3. Most of the class agreed to Sylvia's view that nuclear proliferation is
    potentially a very dangerous problem.

4. What type of a wedding are you planning?

5. I intend on writing letters to my representatives in Congress demanding
    that they do something about homelessness in this state.

EXERCISE W4-4   Clichés and mixed figures of speech   If
you have problems with this exercise, see pp. 78–80 in *A Writer's
Reference*, Second Edition.

Edit the following sentences to replace worn-out expressions and clarify mixed
figures of speech. Revisions of lettered sentences appear in the back of the booklet.
Example:

When he heard about the accident, ~~he turned white as a sheet.~~ *the color drained from his face.*

a. His fellow club members deliberated very briefly; all agreed that his
   behavior was unacceptable beyond the shadow of a doubt.

b. The president thought that the scientists were using science as a
   sledgehammer to grind their political axes.

c. Architect I. M. Pei gave our city a cultural shot in the arm that rubbed off in
   other areas.

d. We ironed out the sticky spots in our relationship.

e. Mel told us that he wasn't willing to put his neck out on a limb.

1. I could read him like a book; he had egg all over his face.

2. Tears were strolling down the child's face.

3. High school is a seething caldron of raw human emotion.

4. There are too many cooks in the broth here at corporate headquarters.

5. Once she had sunk her teeth into it, Helen burned through the assignment.

GRAMMATICAL SENTENCES

EXERCISE G1-1 Subject-verb agreem
problems with this exercise, see pp. 85–91
Second Edition.

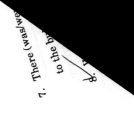

Underline the subject (or compound subject) and then
with it. (If you have difficulty identifying the subject, co
tered sentences appear in the back of the booklet. Exam

> ✓ **Someone** in the audience (has/have) volunteere   ...cipate in the
> **experiment.**

a. Your friendship over the years and your support on a wide variety of
   national issues (has/have) meant a great deal to us.

b. Two-week-old onion rings in the ashtray (is/are) not a pretty sight.

c. Each of these court documents (has/have) been carefully proofread by two
   readers.

d. The main source of income for Trinidad (is/are) oil and pitch.

e. We felt especially confined because there (was/were) no windows in the
   classroom.

1. Neither my cousin nor his rowdy friends (was/were) accused of the prank.

2. Quilts made by the Amish (commands/command) high prices.

3. Sitting in the back seat of the car parked in the driveway (was/were) John
   and the class clown, Philip.

4. The most significant lifesaving device in automobiles (is/are) seatbelts.

5. The old iron gate and the brick wall (makes/make) our courthouse appear
   older than its fifty years.

6. The dangers of smoking (is/are) well documented.

e) a Peanuts cartoon and a few Mother Goose rhymes pinned

lletin board.

hen food supplies (was/were) scarce, the slaves had to make do with the

less desirable parts of the animals.

9. The slaughter of pandas for their much-sought-after pelts (has/have) caused

the panda population to decline dramatically.

10. Zena's family (realizes/realize) that repaying these debts will be difficult.

EXERCISE G1-2   Subject-verb agreement   If you have
problems with this exercise, see pp. 85–91 in *A Writer's Reference*,
Second Edition.

Edit the following sentences for problems with subject-verb agreement. If a sentence is correct, write "correct" after it. Answers to lettered sentences appear in the back of the booklet. Example:

> *were*
> ▷ Jack's first days in the infantry ~~was~~ grueling.
> ∧

a. High concentrations of carbon monoxide results in headaches, dizziness,

unconsciousness, and even death.

b. Not until my interview with Dr. Harvey were other possibilities opened to

me.

c. After hearing the evidence and the closing arguments, the jury was

sequestered.

d. Crystal chandeliers, polished floors, and a new oil painting has transformed

Sandra's apartment.

e. Either Alice or Jan usually work the midnight shift.

1. The board of directors, most of whose members were appointed by the mayor, have just released a report on affirmative action.

2. Of particular concern are penicillin and tetracycline, antibiotics used to make animals more resistant to disease.

3. The presence of certain bacteria in our bodies is one of the factors that determine our overall health.

4. Nearly everyone on the panel favor the arms control agreement.

5. Every year a number of kokanee salmon, not native to the region, is introduced into Flathead Lake.

6. Until recently, economics was not considered a major academic field.

7. All of the witnesses claimed that neither Tom nor his partner was at the scene of the crime.

8. Steve Winwood, as well as Paul Simon, were attending the Grammy Awards ceremony.

9. SEACON is the only one of our war games that emphasize scientific and technical issues.

10. The key program of Alcoholics Anonymous are the twelve steps to recovery.

EXERCISE G1-3   Subject-verb agreement   If you have problems with this exercise, see pp. 85–91 in *A Writer's Reference*, Second Edition.

In the following paragraphs, circle the verb in parentheses that agrees with its subject.

Natalie, together with many other students in her educational philosophy class, (supports/support) a program to standardize cultural literacy in the high school curriculum. Natalie and those who agree with her (argues/argue) that students should have a broad background of shared knowledge. This shared knowledge (helps/help) bind a culture together and (encourages/encourage) pride in our country's heritage. In deciding which knowledge to include in a standardized curriculum, advocates of cultural literacy (looks/look) primarily to the past: If a book (has/have) stood the test of time, they say, it is a part of our culture worth preserving.

Kimberly and several other students in the class (opposes/oppose) the idea of a standardized high school curriculum. They argue that the content of such a curriculum is not easily determined in a multicultural society, especially in subjects such as sociology, history, and literature that (examines/examine) values and beliefs. Kimberly and other opponents of cultural literacy (believes/believe) that knowledge survives over time because a dominant culture preserves it. Kimberly (doesn't/don't) question the value of that knowledge, but she recognizes that the dominant culture over the years (neglects/neglect) to preserve and transmit knowledge that is important to less powerful cultures. The important factor in this debate (is/are) the students: each of them (deserves/deserve) attention and respect. Kimberly worries that plans to standardize cultural literacy (ignores/ignore) the cultures of too many students. She represents those in her class who (feels/feel) that a true cultural literacy program has to include knowledge from many cultures and that standardizing a multicultural curriculum may not be practical on any large scale.

Edit the following sentences for problems with irregular verbs. If a sentence is correct, write "correct" after it. Answers to lettered sentences appear in the back of the booklet. Example:

> Was it you I ~~seen~~ *saw* last night at the concert?

a. Noticing that my roommate was shivering and looking pale, I rung *rang* for the nurse.

b. When I get the urge to exercise, I lay down until it passes.

c. On our way to the airport we realized that Bob had forgotten to pick up our passports from the hotel.

d. The team of engineers watched in horror as the newly built dam burst and flooded the small valley.

e. The young girl looked soulfully into her mother's eyes as she laid the wheezing puppy on its mat.

1. How many times have you swore to yourself, "I'll diet tomorrow, after one more piece of cheesecake"?

2. Laying there in a bed of wet leaves with mist falling lightly on my face, I could hear Linda call my name, but I never answered, not even to say I was alive.

3. My aunt may be poor, but she has always took care of her family.

4. When Sarah saw Mr. Johnson coming home from the corner store, she ran over to him to see if he had brung her some candy.

5. All parents were asked to send a mat for their children to lay on.

6. Lincoln took good care of his legal clients; the contracts he drew for the Illinois Central Railroad could never be broke.

7. Have you ever dreamed that you were falling from a cliff or flying through the air?

8. I locked my brakes, leaned the motorcycle to the left, and laid it down to keep from slamming into the fence.

9. In her junior year, Cindy run the 440-yard dash in 51.1 seconds.

10. Larry claimed that he had drank a bad soda, but Grandmother suspected the truth.

EXERCISE G2-2 -s and -ed verb forms and omitted verbs   If you have problems with this exercise, see pp. 95–98 in *A Writer's Reference*, Second Edition.

Edit the following sentences for problems with -s and -ed verb forms and for omitted verbs. If a sentence is correct, write "correct" after it. Answers to lettered sentences appear in the back of the booklet. Example:

The psychologist ~~have~~ *has* so many problems in her own life that she ~~don't~~ *doesn't*

know how to advise anyone else.

a. I love to watch Anthony as he leaps off the balance beam and lands lightly on his feet.

b. The police are use to helping lost tourists.

c. The whooping crane have been an endangered species since the late 1930s.

d. We often don't know whether he angry or just joking.

e. Staggered working hours have reduce traffic jams and save motorists many gallons of gas.

1. Even though Maria is in her late twenties, her mother treat her like a child.

2. Have there ever been a time in your life when you were too depressed to get out of bed?

3. Many people in my hometown have been ask to help with the rally.

4. Today a modern school building covers most of the old grounds.

5. Chris didn't know about Marlo's death because he never listens. He always talking.

6. That line of poetry can be express more dramatically.

7. Our four children plays one or two instruments each.

8. The ball was pass from one player to the other so fast that even the TV crew miss some of the exchanges.

9. Do he have enough energy to hold down two jobs while going to night school?

10. How would you feel if your mother or a love one had been a victim of a crime like this?

EXERCISE G2-3   Verb tense and mood   If you have problems with this exercise, see pp. 98–100 in *A Writer's Reference*, Second Edition.

Edit the following sentences to eliminate errors in verb tense or mood. If a sentence is correct, write "correct" after it. Answers to lettered sentences appear in the back of the booklet. Example:

had been
After the path ~~was~~ plowed, we were able to walk through the park.
        ∧

a. The fire was thought to have been started around nine o'clock.

b. Watson and Crick discovered the mechanism that controlled inheritance in all life: the workings of the DNA molecule.

c. Marion would write more if she wasn't distracted by a house full of children.

d. Sharon told me that she went to the meeting the day before.

e. Ken recommended that John remain on the beginners' slope for at least a week.

1. Dad called in the morning and said that he took Mom to the hospital around midnight.

2. They had planned to have adopted a girl, but they got twin boys.

3. If I were in better health, I would enjoy competing in the dance marathon.

4. As soon as my aunt applied for the position of assistant pastor, the post was filled by an inexperienced seminary graduate who had been so hastily snatched that his mortarboard was still in midair.

5. Sheila knew that Bruce would have preferred to have double-dated, but she really wanted to be alone with him.

6. Don Quixote, in Cervantes' novel, was an idealist ill suited for life in the real world.

7. On arrival at the police station, Cindy pulled Tom out of the car, and he had fallen face down on the ground.

8. I would like to have been on the *Mayflower* but not to have lived through that first winter.

9. On the very day that Alex signed up for the marines, his girlfriend had joined the navy.

10. Hearing the screams and wondering whether Chuck had had an accident, I

ran to the garage.

EXERCISE G2-4   Active and passive voice   If you have
problems with this exercise, see p. 101 in *A Writer's Reference*,
Second Edition.

In the following paragraphs, the italicized passive verbs are less effective than active verbs would be. Replace each italicized passive verb with an active verb. Be prepared to discuss why the remaining passive verbs (printed in brackets) are appropriate.

Although Professor Whist works as a consultant for several corporations that

manufacture electrical generating equipment, he [is known and respected] by

environmentalists as an advocate for the preservation of natural resources.

Professor Whist feels that his influence *can be used* to affect corporate decisions

concerning the environment. The environment *is protected* to some extent by many

corporations, but when someone with Professor Whist's reputation *is hired* by them,

their public image *is improved* too.

Although Professor Whist [is besieged] by many groups for his expertise, he

continues to teach. For part of every class a discussion *is led* about how the

environment *is affected* by everyday decisions of big corporations as well as ordinary

people. Each semester, for example, students learn that electricity [is produced] by

a very inefficient process, with only about 35 percent of the potential energy in coal,

oil, or uranium converting directly into electricity. Students also learn that simple

steps *can be taken* at home to conserve every type of energy that *is used*. Professor

Whist believes that he can make a difference, and his conviction *is demonstrated* by

his personal example in the conference room and in the classroom.

EXERCISE G3-1   Pronoun-antecedent agreement   If you
have problems with this exercise, see pp. 102–04 in *A Writer's
Reference*, Second Edition.

Edit the following sentences to eliminate problems with pronoun-antecedent agreement. Most of the sentences can be revised in more than one way, so experiment
before choosing a solution. If a sentence is correct, write "correct" after it. Revisions
of lettered sentences appear in the back of the booklet. Example:

> *Recruiters*
> ~~The recruiter~~ may tell the truth, but there is much that they choose
> ∧
> not to tell.

a. Anyone who is taking the school bus to the volleyball game must bring in a
    permission slip signed by their parents.

b. The sophomore class elects its president tomorrow.

c. Late at night, I sometimes saw a priest or a brother entering the side door of
    the church, their faces silhouetted briefly in the moonlight.

d. A climatologist collects weather data from around the world. They then
    analyze the data and pass their analyses along to forecasters.

e. If you have anyone attending class who is still not on your roster, please
    send them to the registration office.

1. If a driver refuses to take a blood or breath test, he or she will have their
    licenses suspended for six months.

2. Why should we care about the timber wolf? One answer is that they have
    proven beneficial to humans by killing off weakened prey.

3. No one should be forced to sacrifice their prized possession — life — for
    someone else.

34   *G3-1 • Pronoun-antecedent agreement*

4. Everyone who enjoys freedom should recognize their indebtedness to the founders of our country.

5. The navy has much to offer any man or woman who knows what they want.

6. The committee plans to distribute copies of their proposal on Monday.

7. David lent his motorcycle to someone who allowed their friend to use it.

8. By the final curtain, 90 percent of the audience had voted with their feet.

9. A mountain climber must shift his or her emphasis from self-preservation to group survival. They must learn to rely completely on others.

10. A graduate student needs to be willing to take on a sizable debt unless they have wealthy families.

EXERCISE G3-2 Pronoun-antecedent agreement If you have problems with this exercise, see pp. 102–04 in *A Writer's Reference*, Second Edition.

Edit the following paragraphs for problems with pronoun-antecedent agreement. Choose an effective revision strategy that avoids sexist language.

John found himself surrounded by students who were returning to college after an absence of more than fifteen years, and they shared his nervousness. No one knew what changes they should expect. Because Alice and David had been in the same situation last year, Dean Shell asked each of them to share their experiences during an orientation workshop. Neither John nor the other older students allowed his schedule to interfere with the workshop.

David mentioned that the biggest surprise for him had been the extensive use of computers. Fifteen years ago, he recalled, a math student rarely did their homework on a computer. Now, he said, no one has to do their assignments without the help of a software program. David asked the audience if it remembered erasable bond paper and correction tape, and they groaned, recalling the frustration of typing term papers. Now, said David, a student can write their papers in the campus computer labs.

Alice said that a returning student would also be surprised when they saw how the course content had changed. Every department, she said, had found their own way of incorporating the work of women and minorities in their courses. And almost all the departments had pooled their resources to create interdisciplinary courses. A student shouldn't be surprised, Alice said, to find a novel assigned in their sociology class or an oral history project featured in their English class. A final surprise, Alice noted, is the extent to which writing is now emphasized across the curriculum — in the sciences, the social sciences, and even math.

After hearing David and Alice share their positive experience, the audience felt that many of its fears were unfounded, and they looked forward to the coming semesters.

EXERCISE G3-3   Pronoun reference   If you have problems with this exercise, see pp. 104–06 in *A Writer's Reference*, Second Edition.

Edit the following sentences to correct errors in pronoun reference. In some cases you will need to decide on an antecedent that the pronoun might logically refer to. Revisions of lettered sentences appear in the back of the booklet. Example:

> Following the breakup of AT&T, many other companies began to offer
> *The competition*
> long-distance phone service. ~~This~~ has led to lower long-distance
> ∧
> rates.

a.   The detective removed the blood-stained shawl from the body and then photographed it.

---

b. In Professor Johnson's class, you are lucky to earn a C.

c. Satanism is a serious problem in our country. Their rites are grotesque perversions of many of Christianity's sacred rituals.

d. The Comanche braves' lifestyle was particularly violent; they gained respect for their skill as warriors.

e. All students can secure parking permits from the campus police office; they are open from 8 A.M. until 8 P.M.

1. The racetrack is well equipped for emergencies. They even have an ambulance at the track on racing days.

2. Many people believe that the polygraph test is highly reliable if you employ a licensed examiner.

3. We expected the concert to last for at least two hours. Since the average ticket sells for twenty dollars, this was not being unrealistic.

4. In Camilla's autobiography, she revealed the story behind her short stay in prison.

5. In the encyclopedia it states that male moths can smell female moths from several miles away.

6. When Aunt Harriet put the cake on the table, it collapsed.

7. Employees are beginning to take advantage of the company's athletic facilities. They offer squash and tennis courts, a small track, and several trampolines.

8. Be sure to visit Istanbul's bazaar, where they sell everything from Persian rugs to electronic calculators.

9. If an accountant makes errors regularly, it will cause him or her to be put on

   probation.

10. My favorite newscasters are those which reveal their point of view.

EXERCISE G3-4   Pronoun case: personal pronouns   If you
have problems with this exercise, see pp. 106–10 in *A Writer's
Reference*, Second Edition.

Edit the following sentences to eliminate errors in case. If a sentence is correct,
write "correct" after it. Answers to lettered sentences appear in the back of the booklet. Example:

he,

Grandfather cuts down trees for neighbors much younger than ~~him.~~
                                                                       ∧

a. My Ethiopian neighbor was puzzled by the dedication of we joggers.

b. Andrea whispered, "Who's there?" and Alfred replied softly that it was he.

c. Sue's husband is ten years older than her.

d. The winners, Julie and him, were unable to attend the awards ceremony.

e. The chances against you getting hit by lightning are about two million to

   one.

1. Doctors should take more seriously what us patients say about our

   treatment.

2. Grandfather said he would give anything to live nearer to Paulette and me.

3. Maxine did not do well on her medical boards because her and her tutor had

   spent the night before the exam worrying rather than reviewing.

4. A professional counselor advised the division chief that Marco, Fidelia, and

   myself should be allowed to apply for the opening.

---

5. Because of last night's fire, we are fed up with him drinking and smoking.

6. The governor granted David and I pardons on January 2, 1990.

7. The swirling cyclone caused he and his horse to race for shelter.

8. The four candidates — Paul, Erica, Tracy, and I — will participate in tonight's televised debate.

9. During the testimony the witness pointed directly at the defendant and announced that the thief was him.

10. When in Aruba, Marlena bought several shell paintings for Donelle and I.

EXERCISE G3-5 **Pronoun case: *who* and *whom***   If you have problems with this exercise, see pp. 110–11 in *A Writer's Reference*, Second Edition.

Edit the following sentences to eliminate errors in the use of *who* and *whom* (or *whoever* and *whomever*). If a sentence is correct, write "correct" after it. Answers to lettered sentences appear in the back of the booklet. Example:

> *whom*
> **What is the name of the person ~~who~~ you are sponsoring for**
> **   ∧**
> **membership in the club?**

a. In his first production of *Hamlet,* who did Laurence Olivier replace?

b. Who was Martin Luther King's mentor?

c. Datacall allows you to talk to whoever needs you no matter where you are in the building.

d. Some group leaders cannot handle the pressure; they give whomever makes the most noise most of their attention.

e. One of the women who Johnson hired became the most successful lawyer in the agency.

1. The shift supervisor will ask you to relieve whoever needs a break.

2. When medicine is scarce and expensive, physicians must give it to whomever has the best chance to survive.

3. Now that you have seen both fighters in action, who in your opinion will win the championship?

4. Mr. Barnes is the elementary schoolteacher who I recall most fondly.

5. Who was accused of receiving Mafia funds?

6. They will become business partners with whomever is willing to contribute to the company's coffers.

7. The only interstate travelers who get pulled over for speeding are the ones whom cannot afford a radar detector.

8. The elderly woman who I was asked to take care of was a clever, delightful companion.

9. The teacher often calls on whoever does not raise a hand.

10. Who should Howard see about the tickets?

EXERCISE G3-6 Pronoun case   If you have problems with this exercise, see pp. 106–11 in *A Writer's Reference*, Second Edition.

Edit the following paragraph to correct errors in case. (See G3-c and G3-d.)

After our freshman year, my friend Kim and me were trying to decide if we wanted to major in business administration. Dr. Bane, an economics professor who we had first semester, agreed to talk with Kim and I. At first, Kim did not seem as interested in a business career as I, but then Dr. Bane explained to us neophytes how many options are open to business graduates. Neither Kim nor myself had realized that the possibilities are so interesting, Dr. Bane told us about a recent graduate whom he felt was one of his most promising students: She owns and manages her own bookstore. Another recent graduate, who Dr. Bane almost flunked senior year, is a buyer for a chain of clothing stores. Dr. Bane was surprised at him becoming successful so soon, but he said there's a niche for everyone in business. Dr. Bane cautioned us with a story about another graduate who was interested only in whomever would pay her the most. "Money isn't everything," Dr. Bane said. "Your being well matched to your work is more important than earning large sums of money." He then invited us, both Kim and I, to his senior seminar in which students discuss their internships. When we thanked Dr. Bane for his advice, he told Kim and me that it probably would not be hard for we too to find our niche in business.

EXERCISE G4-1   Adjectives and adverbs   If you have problems with this exercise, see pp. 111–15 in *A Writer's Reference*, Second Edition.

Edit the following sentences to eliminate errors in the use of adjectives and adverbs. If a sentence is correct, write "correct" after it. Answers to lettered sentences appear in the back of the booklet. Example:

When I watched Carl run the 440 on Saturday, I was amazed at how
well
~~good~~ **he paced himself.**
∧

a. My mechanic showed me exactly where to wrap the wire firm around the muffler.

b. All of us on the team felt badly about our performance.

c. My mother thinks that Carmen is the most pleasant of the twins.

d. The vaulting box, commonly known as the horse, is the easiest of the four pieces of equipment to master.

e. Last Christmas was the most perfect day of my life.

1. When answering the phone, you should speak clearly and courteous.

2. Which restaurant do you think makes the better hamburger, McDonald's, Burger King, or Wendy's?

3. We wanted a hunting dog. We didn't care if he smelled badly, but we really did not want him to smell bad.

4. We were real surprised to hear that Uncle Bob had been nominated for a Nobel Prize.

5. The union contract may make all first-year teachers equal, but it does not make them equally effective.

6. The manager must see that the office runs smooth and efficient.

7. Professor Brown's public praise of my performance on the exam made me feel a little strangely.

8. Of all my relatives, Uncle Robert is the most cleverest.

9. The hall closet is so filled with ski equipment that the door won't hardly close.

10. Marcia performed very well at her Drama Club audition.

EXERCISE G5-1   Sentence fragments   If you have problems
with this exercise, see pp. 115–18 in *A Writer's Reference*, Second
Edition.

Repair any fragment by attaching it to a nearby sentence or by rewriting it as a
complete sentence. If a word group is correct, write "correct" after it. Revisions of
lettered sentences appear in the back of the booklet. Example:

> **One Greek island that should not be missed is Mykonos, A vacation**
>
> **spot for Europeans and a playpen for the rich.**

a. As I stood in front of the microwave, I recalled my grandmother bending

over her old black stove. And remembered what she taught me: that any food

can have soul if you love the people you are cooking for.

b. It has been said that there are only three indigenous American art forms.

Jazz, musical comedy, and soap opera.

c. I stepped on some frozen moss and started sliding down the face of a flat

rock toward the falls. Suddenly I landed on another rock.

d. Myra did not tell us about her new job for six weeks. Although she saw one

or the other of us every day.

e. While on a tour of Italy, Maria and Kathleen sneaked away from their group

to spend some quiet minutes with Leonardo da Vinci's *Last Supper.* A

stunning fresco painted in the fifteenth century in a Milan monastery.

1. Recently I visited a friend who was confined in Occoquan II. A correctional

facility located in Lorton, Virginia.

2. Mother loved to play all our favorite games. Canasta, Monopoly,

hide-and-seek, and even kick the can.

3. Underneath all his brashness, Henry is really a thoughtful person. Few of his colleagues realize how sensitive he is.

4. I had pushed these fears into one of those quiet places in my mind. Hoping they would stay there asleep.

5. To give my family a comfortable, secure home life. That is my most important goal.

6. If a woman from the desert tribe showed anger toward her husband, she was whipped in front of the whole village. And shunned by the rest of the women.

7. A tornado is a violent whirling wind. One that produces a funnel-shaped cloud and moves over land in a narrow path of destruction.

8. With machetes, the explorers cut their way through the tall grasses to the edge of the canyon. Where they began to lay out their tapes for the survey.

9. Bill is a disciplined yet adventurous player. Unlike his brother Ken.

10. Theodosia had hated her name for as long as she could remember. Because it sounded so old-fashioned.

EXERCISE G5-2 Sentence fragments   If you have problems with this exercise, see pp. 115–18 in *A Writer's Reference,* Second Edition.

Repair each fragment in the following paragraphs by attaching it to a sentence nearby or by rewriting it as a complete sentence.

Until recently, Maria thought that studying a foreign language would not be very useful. Because she was going to be a business major, training for management. Even if she worked for a company with an office overseas, she was

---

sure that international clients would communicate in English. The accepted language of the world marketplace. But Maria's adviser, Professor Will, told her that many U.S. firms are owned by foreign corporations. Or rely on the sales of subsidiaries in foreign markets. English is therefore not always the language of preference.

Professor Will advised Maria to learn a foreign language. Such as French, German, or Japanese. These are the most useful languages, he told her. In addition to preparing her to use the language, the classes would expose her to the history, culture, and politics of another country. Factors that often affect business decisions. After talking with Professor Will, Maria was convinced. To begin immediately to prepare for her business career by studying a foreign language.

EXERCISE G6-1   Comma splices and fused sentences   If you have problems with this exercise, see pp. 119–22 in *A Writer's Reference,* Second Edition.

Revise any comma splices or fused sentences using the method of revision suggested in brackets. Revisions of lettered sentences appear in the back of the booklet. Example:

Because
∧**Orville was obsessed with his weight, he rarely ate anything sweet and delicious.** [*Restructure the sentence.*]

a. The city had one public swimming pool, it stayed packed with children all summer long. [*Restructure the sentence.*]

b. Most parents want their children to do well in school, however, they don't always know how to help them succeed. [*Use a comma and a coordinating conjunction.*]

---

c. Why should we pay taxes to support public transportation, we prefer to save energy dollars by carpooling. [*Make two sentences.*]

d. Suddenly there was a loud silence, the shelling had stopped. [*Use a semicolon.*]

e. As I walked into the living room, a special report flashed onto the TV screen, the space shuttle had exploded. [*Use a colon.*]

1. For the first time in her adult life, Lisa had time to waste, she could spend a whole day curled up with a good book. [*Use a semicolon.*]

2. It is impossible for parents to monitor all the television their children see, therefore, many parents just give up and offer no supervision at all. [*Restructure the sentence.*]

3. The next time an event is canceled because of bad weather, don't blame the meteorologist, blame nature. [*Make two sentences.*]

4. While we were walking down Grover Avenue, Gary told us about his Aunt Elsinia, she was an extraordinary woman. [*Restructure the sentence.*]

5. The president of Algeria was standing next to the podium he was waiting to be introduced. [*Restructure the sentence.*]

6. On most days I had only enough money for bus fare, lunch was a luxury I could not afford. [*Use a semicolon.*]

7. There was one major reason for John's wealth, his grandfather had been a multimillionaire. [*Use a colon.*]

8. John positioned himself next to the smartest girl in class, he wouldn't cheat, of course, but it was comforting to know that the right answer was not far away. [*Make two sentences.*]

9. It was too late to catch a bus after the party, therefore, four of us pooled our money and called a cab. [*Use a comma and a coordinating conjunction.*]

10. Wind power for the home is a supplementary source of energy, it can be combined with electricity, gas, or solar energy. [*Restructure the sentence.*]

EXERCISE G6-2 Comma splices and fused sentences If you have problems with this exercise, see pp. 119–22 in *A Writer's Reference,* Second Edition.

Revise any comma splices or fused sentences using a technique that you find effective. If a sentence is correct, write "correct" after it. Revisions of lettered sentences appear in the back of the booklet. Example:

but
I ran the three blocks as fast as I could, however I still missed the bus.
∧

a. The trail up Mount Finegold was declared impassable, therefore, we decided to return to our hotel a day early.

b. The duck hunter set out his decoys in the shallow bay and then settled in to wait for the first real bird to alight.

c. The officer must enforce the laws, this is true even when the laws seem unfair.

d. Researchers were studying the fertility of Texas land tortoises they X-rayed all the female tortoises to see how many eggs they had.

e. The suburbs seemed cold, they lacked the warmth and excitement of our Italian neighborhood.

1. Are you able to endure boredom, isolation, and potential violence, then the army may well be the adventure for you.

---

2. Maria gave her mother half of her weekly pay then she used the rest as a down payment on a stereo system at Brown's Sounds.

3. If one of the dogs should happen to fall through the ice, it would be cut loose from the team and left to its fate, the sled drivers could not endanger the rest of the team for just one dog.

4. The volunteers worked hard to clean up and restore calm after the tornado, as a matter of fact, many of them did not sleep for the first three days of the emergency.

5. Taking drugs to keep alert on the job or in school can actually cause a decline in work performance and lead to severe depression as well.

6. Pablo had not prepared well for his first overseas assignment, but luck was with him, he performed better than the more experienced members of his unit.

7. It was obvious that Susan had already been out walking in the woods, her boots were covered with mud and leaves.

8. We didn't trust her, she had lied before.

9. I pushed open the first door with my back, turning to open the second door, I encountered a young woman in a wheelchair holding it open for me.

10. If you want to lose weight and keep it off, consider this advice, don't try to take it off faster than you put it on.

In the following rough draft, repair any sentence fragments and revise any comma splices or fused sentences.

Teri, Karen, and I took introductory foreign language courses last year. Each of us was interested in learning a different language, however, we were all trying to accomplish the same goal. To begin mastering a new language. When we compared our classes and the results, we found that each course used a quite different approach to language learning.

In my Spanish course, Professor Cruz introduced lists of new vocabulary words every week, she devoted half of each class to grammar rules. I spent most of my time memorizing lists and rules. In addition to vocabulary and grammar study, I read passages of Spanish literature. Translating them into English. And wrote responses to the reading in Spanish. The only time I spoke Spanish, however, was when I translated a passage or answered questions in class. Although Professor Cruz spoke Spanish for the entire class period.

Instead of memorizing vocabulary lists and grammar rules and translating reading selections, Teri's Portuguese class rehearsed simple dialogues useful for tourists. Conducting every class in Portuguese, Teri's professor asked students to recite the dialogues, she corrected the students' pronunciation and grammar as they spoke. Teri's homework was to go to the language lab, she listened to various dialogues and practiced ordering meals, asking for directions to a train station, and so on. Teri learned to pronounce the language well, she mastered the simple dialogues. But she did not get much practice in reading.

Karen took a course in Russian, her experience was different from Teri's and from mine. Her professor asked the students to read articles from the Soviet press.

And to listen to recent news programs from the Soviet Union. In class, students discussed the articles and programs. Teri's professor encouraged the students to use Russian as much as possible in their discussions, she also allowed them to use English. Other class activities included writing letters in response to articles in Soviet publications and role playing to duplicate real-life situations. Such as a discussion with a neighbor about the lack of meat in the shops. Karen learned to understand spoken Russian and to speak the language, in addition, she regularly practiced reading and writing. Although her Russian course was difficult, Karen thinks it will help her when she visits the Soviet Union this summer.

Of the three of us, Karen is the most positive about her course. She is certain that she will further develop her language skills when visiting the Soviet Union, moreover, she is confident that she can communicate without struggling too much with a dictionary. Teri and I feel less positive about our courses. Because we both have forgotten the vocabulary and grammar rules. If I were asked to read a passage in Spanish now, I couldn't, Teri says she would not understand Portuguese or be able to respond to a single dialogue if she had to.

ESL TROUBLE SPOTS

EXERCISE T1-1 Articles If you have problems with this exercise, see pp. 125–28 in *A Writer's Reference*, Second Edition.

Articles have been omitted from the following story, adapted from *Zen Flesh, Zen Bones*, compiled by Paul Reps. Insert the articles *a, an,* and *the* where English requires them and be prepared to explain the reasons for your choices.

Moon Cannot Be Stolen

Ryokan, who was Zen master, lived simple life in little hut at foot of mountain.

One evening thief visited hut only to discover there was nothing in it to steal.

Ryokan returned and caught him. "You may have come long way to visit me," he told prowler, "and you should not return empty-handed. Please take my clothes as gift." Thief was bewildered. He took Ryokan's clothes and slunk away. Ryokan sat naked, watching moon. "Poor fellow," he mused, "I wish I could give him this beautiful moon."

EXERCISE T2-1   Helping verbs and main verbs   If you have problems with this exercise, see pp. 128–31 in *A Writer's Reference,* Second Edition.

Revise any sentences in which helping and main verbs do not match. You may need to look at the list of irregular verbs in G2-a to determine the correct form of some irregular verbs. Answers to lettered sentences appear in the back of the booklet. Example:

Maureen should find̸ an apartment closer to campus.

a.   We will making this a better country.

b.   There is nothing in the world that TV has not touch on.

c.   Did you understood my question?

d.   A hard wind was blown while we were climbing the mountain.

e.   The child's innocent world has been taking away from him.

1.   Children are expose at an early age to certain aspects of adult life.

2.   The student can't concentrated on his lessons.

3.   Can you told me the time?

4.   I have ate Thai food only once before.

5.   Sandra says that she doesn't wants any help.

Edit the following conditional sentences for problems with verbs. In some cases, more than one revision is possible. Possible answers to lettered sentences appear in the back of the booklet. Example:

> If I ~~have~~ the money, I would meet my friends in Barcelona next summer.

with *had* written above the struck-out *have*.

a. If I had the money, I would have met my friends in Barcelona last summer.

b. If Martin Luther King, Jr., was alive today, he would be appalled by the violence in our inner cities.

c. Whenever my uncle comes to visit, he brought me an expensive present.

d. We will lose our largest client unless we would update our computer system.

e. If Virginia wins a fellowship, she would go to graduate school.

1. If it would not be raining, we could go fishing.

2. If Lee had followed the doctor's orders, he had recovered from his operation by now.

3. You would have met my cousin if you came to the party last night.

4. Whenever I washed my car, it rains.

5. Our daughter would have drowned if Officer Blake didn't risk his life to save her.

EXERCISE T2-3 Verbs followed by gerunds or infinitives
If you have problems with this exercise, see pp. 133–35 in *A Writer's Reference,* Second Edition.

Form sentences by adding gerund or infinitive constructions to the following sentence openings. In some cases, more than one kind of construction may be possible. Possible sentences for lettered items appear in the back of the booklet. Example:

Please remind your sister to call me.

a. I enjoy

b. Will you help Samantha

c. The team hopes

d. Tom and his brothers miss

e. The babysitter let

1. Pollen makes

2. The club president asked

3. Next summer we plan

4. Waverly intends

5. Please stop

EXERCISE T3-1   Omissions and repetitions
If you have problems with this exercise, see pp. 137–39 in *A Writer's Reference,* Second Edition.

In the following sentences, add needed subjects, expletives, or verbs, and delete any repeated subjects, objects, or adverbs. Answers to lettered sentences appear in the back of the booklet. Example:

Nancy is the woman whom I talked to ~~her~~ last week.

a. Is easy to learn how to operate our computers.

b. My grandfather very old-fashioned.

c. The prime minister she is the most popular leader in my country.

d. Pavel hasn't heard from the cousin whom he wrote to her last month.

e. Are many skyscrapers in New York City.

1. Henri and Nicole they are good friends.

2. Is important to study the grammar of English.

3. The neighbor we trusted he was a thief.

4. I don't use the subway because am afraid.

5. Archeologists have excavated the city where the old Persian kings are

   buried there.

EXERCISE T3-2   Order of cumulative adjectives   If you have problems with this exercise, see pp. 139–41 in *A Writer's Reference,* Second Edition.

Arrange the following modifiers and nouns in their proper order. Answers to lettered items appear in the back of the booklet. Example:

two new French racing bicycles
new, French, two, bicycles, racing

a. woman, young, an, Vietnamese, attractive

b. dedicated, a, priest, Catholic

c. old, her, sweater, blue, wool

---

d. delicious, Joe's, Scandinavian, bread

e. many, cages, bird, antique, beautiful

1. round, two, marble, tables, large

2. several, yellow, tulips, miniature

3. a, sports, classic, car

4. courtyard, a, square, small, brick

5. charming, restaurants, Italian, several

EXERCISE T3-3 **Present versus past participles** If you
have problems with this exercise, see pp. 141–42 in *A Writer's
Reference*, Second Edition.

Edit the following sentences for proper use of present and past participles. Do not
change correct sentences. Answers to lettered sentences appear in the back of the
booklet. Example:

> *excited*
> **Danielle and Monica were very ~~exciting~~ to be going to a Broadway**
> ∧
> **show for the first time.**

a. My mother was annoying at me for coming home late.

b. The noise in the hall was distracted to me.

c. After the overnight trip to Washington, Samuel was exhausted.

d. The violence in recent movies is often disgusted.

e. I have never seen anyone as surprised as Mona when she walked through

   the door and we turned on the lights.

---

1. Megan worked on her art project for eight hours but still she was not satisfying.

2. That blackout was the most frightened experience I've ever had.

3. I couldn't concentrate on my homework because I was distracted.

4. Psalm 23 is one of the most uplifting pieces of writing I've ever read.

5. The exhibit on the La Brea tar pits was fascinated.

PUNCTUATION

EXERCISE P1-1 The comma: independent clauses, introductory elements   If you have problems with this exercise, see pp. 145–46 in *A Writer's Reference*, Second Edition.

Add or delete commas where necessary in the following sentences. If a sentence is correct, write "correct" after it. Answers to lettered sentences appear in the back of the booklet. Example:

Because it rained all Labor Day, our picnic was rather soggy.
                                          ∧

a. Carla didn't know whether to punish the boy for lying or praise him for being so clever.

b. The man at the next table complained loudly and the waiter stomped off in disgust.

c. Instead of eating half a cake or two dozen cookies I now grab a banana or an orange.

d. Nursing is physically, and mentally demanding, yet the pay is low.

e. After I won the hundred-yard dash I found a bench in the park and collapsed.

✓

1. After everyone had eaten Lu and George cut the cake.

2. He pushed the car beyond the toll gate and poured a bucket of water on the smoking hood.

3. Lighting the area like a second moon the helicopter circled the scene.

4. While one of the robbers tied Laureen to a chair, and gagged her with an apron, the other emptied the contents of the safe into a knapsack.

5. Many musicians of Bach's time played several instruments, but few mastered them as early or played with as much expression as Bach.

EXERCISE P1-2 The comma: series, coordinate adjectives
If you have trouble with this exercise, see pp. 147–48 in *A Writer's Reference,* Second Edition.

Add or delete commas where necessary in the following sentences. If a sentence is correct, write "correct" after it. Answers to lettered sentences appear in the back of the booklet. Example:

We gathered our essentials, took off for the great outdoors‚ and
ignored the fact that it was Friday the 13th.

a. She wore a black silk cape, a rhinestone collar, satin gloves and high tops.

b. I called the fire department, ran downstairs to warn my neighbors, and discovered that they had set the fire on purpose.

c. City Café is noted for its spicy vegetarian dishes and its friendly efficient service.

d. Juan walked through the room with casual elegant grace.

e. My cat's pupils had constricted to small black shining dots.

1. My brother and I found a dead garter snake, picked it up and placed it on Miss Eunice's doorstep.

2. For breakfast the children ordered cornflakes, English muffins with peanut butter and cherry Cokes.

3. With a little ingenuity and a few spices, a good cook can create an appealing variety of nutritious, low-cost meals.

4. Mark was clad in a luminous orange rain suit and a brilliant white helmet.

5. Anne Frank and thousands like her were forced to hide in attics, cellars and secret rooms in an effort to save their lives.

EXERCISE P1-3   The comma: nonrestrictive elements   If you have problems with this exercise, see pp. 148–50 in *A Writer's Reference,* Second Edition.

Add or delete commas where necessary in the following sentences. If a sentence is correct, write "correct" after it. Answers to lettered sentences appear in the back of the booklet. Example:

> My youngest sister, who plays left wing on the team, now lives at
> The Sands, a beach house near Los Angeles.

a. We encountered no problems until we reached Cripple Creek where the trail forked.

b. The Scott Pack which is a twenty-five-pound steel bottle of air is designed to be worn on a firefighter's back.

c. The woman running for the council seat in the fifth district had a long history of community service.

---

d. Shakespeare's tragedy, *King Lear,* was given a splendid perform/

actor, Laurence Olivier.

e. It was a dreary barn of a place located in an even drearier section of town.

1. I had the pleasure of talking to a woman who had just returned from India where she had lived for ten years.

2. Greg's cousin, Albert, lives in Huntington Beach. [*Greg has more than one cousin.*]

3. The gentleman waiting for a prescription is Mr. Riley.

4. *Where the Wild Things Are,* the 1964 Caldecott Medal winner, is my nephew's favorite book.

5. Going on an archeological dig which has always been an ambition of mine seems out of the question this year.

EXERCISE P1-4   Major uses of the comma   If you have problems with this exercise, see pp. 145–50 in *A Writer's Reference,* Second Edition.

This exercise covers the major uses of the comma described in P1-a, b, c, d, and e. Add or delete commas where necessary; do not change correct sentences. Answers to lettered sentences appear in the back of the booklet. Example:

Although we invited him to the party, Gerald decided to spend another late night in the computer room.

a. The whiskey stills which were run mostly by farmers and fishermen were about twenty miles from the nearest town.

. At the sound of a starting pistol the horses surged forward toward the first obstacle, a sharp incline three feet high.

c. Each morning the seventy-year-old woman cleans the barn, shovels manure and spreads clean hay around the milking stalls.

d. The students of Highpoint are required to wear dull green, polyester pleated skirts.

e. You will be unable to answer all the clients' questions or solve all their problems but you may turn to the directory when difficult issues arise.

1. Many Americans prefer Japanese cars which are generally more reliable and a better value than domestic automobiles.

2. Janice's costume was completed with bright red, snakeskin sandals.

3. Siddhartha decided to leave his worldly possessions behind and live in the forest by a beautiful river.

4. The lawyer fully explained the contract, but we weren't certain we understood all of its implications.

5. While hunting with a relative Greg was accidentally shot in the back.

6. Michael Jordan, who was the highest scorer in the game became the National Basketball Association's Most Valuable Player.

7. Aunt Betsy was an impossible, demanding guest.

8. The French *Mirage,* the fastest airplane in the Colombian air force, was an astonishing machine to fly.

9. After being juggled among a dentist, a periodontist and an oral surgeon during the last two years, I have learned to appreciate my teeth.

10. As the summer slowly passed and we came to terms with Mike's death we

    visited the grave site less frequently.

EXERCISE P1-5   All uses of the comma   If you have problems
with this exercise, see pp. 145–54 in *A Writer's Reference,* Second
Edition.

Add or delete commas where necessary in the following sentences; do not change
correct sentences. Answers to lettered sentences appear in the back of the booklet.
Example:

> **"Yes, Virginia, there is a Santa Claus," said the editor.**
>   ∧

a. On January 29, 1990 we finally received Ms. Gilroy's reply to our letter of

    November 16, 1989.

b. The coach having bawled us out thoroughly, we left the locker room with his

    angry harsh words ringing in our ears.

c. Good technique does not guarantee however, that the power you develop will

    be sufficient for Kyok Pa competition.

d. We bought a home in Upper Marlboro where my husband worked as a mail

    carrier.

e. Please make the check payable to David Kerr D.D.S., not David Kerr M.D.

1. Mr. Mundy was born on July 22, 1939 in Arkansas, where his family had

    lived for four generations.

2. It has been reported that the Republican who suggested Eisenhower as a

    presidential candidate meant Milton not Ike.

---

3. Thermography, most experts agree, was safer than early forms of mammography.

4. We pulled into the first apartment complex we saw, and slowly patrolled the parking lots.

5. On Christmas morning, the children wildly excited about their gifts forgot their promise not to wake their parents.

6. I found Bill, my pet piranha, belly up in the tank one day his body floating listlessly in the water.

7. We wondered how our overweight grandmother could have been the pretty bride in the picture, but we kept our wonderings to ourselves.

8. "The last flight" she said with a sigh "went out five minutes before I arrived at the airport."

9. The Rio Grande, the border between Texas and Mexico lay before us. It was a sluggish mud-filled meandering stream that gave off an odor akin to sewage.

10. Julia lives in Sawbridgeworth, Hertfordshire England for most of the year.

EXERCISE P2-1   Unnecessary commas   If you have problems with this exercise, see pp. 155–58 in *A Writer's Reference,* Second Edition.

Delete commas where necessary in the following sentences. If a sentence is correct, write "correct" after it. Answers to lettered sentences appear in the back of the booklet. Example:

Loretta Lynn has paved the way for artists such as/ Reba McEntire and the Judds.

---

a. We'd rather spend our money on blue-chip stocks, than speculate on porkbellies.

b. Being prepared for the worst, is one way to escape disappointment.

c. When he heard the groans, he opened the door, and ran out.

d. My father said, that he would move to California, if I would agree to transfer to UCLA.

e. I quickly accepted the fact that I was, literally, in third-class quarters.

1. Ms. Smith's favorite is the youngest brother, Timmy.

2. He wore a thick, black, wool coat over army fatigues.

3. Often public figures, (Michael Jackson is a good example) go to great lengths to guard their private lives.

4. She loved early spring flowers such as crocuses, daffodils, and snowdrops.

5. Students, who sign up for Children's Literature and expect an easy A, have usually revised their expectations by the end of the first week.

6. Mesquite, the hardest of the softwoods, grows primarily in the Southwest.

7. Dougherty says that the record for arrests would have been better, if he had not pulled the officers away from their regular duties to assist the homicide division.

8. The kitchen was covered with black soot, that had been deposited by the woodburning stove, which stood in the middle of the room.

9. Captain Edward Spurlock observed, that the vast majority of crimes in our city are committed by repeat offenders.

10. Sharecroppers are given a free house, but they pay for everything else.

Add commas or semicolons where needed in the following well-known quotations. If a sentence is correct, write "correct" after it. Answers to lettered sentences appear in the back of the booklet. Example:

> **If an animal does something, we call it instinct; if we do the same thing, we call it intelligence.** — **Will Cuppy**

a. If fifty million people say a foolish thing it is still a foolish thing.

> — Anatole France

b. No amount of experimentation can ever prove me right a single experiment can prove me wrong. — Albert Einstein

c. Don't talk about yourself it will be done when you leave. — Wilson Mizner

d. The only sensible ends of literature are first the pleasurable toil of writing second the gratification of one's family and friends and lastly the solid cash.

> — Nathaniel Hawthorne

e. All animals are equal but some animals are more equal than others.

> — George Orwell

1. Everyone is a genius at least once a year a real genius has his [or her] original ideas closer together. — G.C. Lichtenberg

2. When choosing between two evils I always like to try the one I've never tried before. — Mae West

3. I don't know who my grandfather was I am much more concerned to know what his grandson will be. — Abraham Lincoln

4. America is a country that doesn't know where it is going but is determined

   to set a speed record getting there.   — Lawrence J. Peter

5. I've been rich and I've been poor; rich is better.   — Sophie Tucker

---

EXERCISE P3-2   The semicolon and the comma   If you have problems with this exercise, see pp. 158–61 in *A Writer's Reference,* Second Edition.

Edit the following sentences to correct errors in the use of the comma and the semicolon. If a sentence is correct, write "correct" after it. Answers to lettered sentences appear in the back of the booklet. Example:

Love is blind; envy has its eyes wide open.
          ∧

a. For some, happiness comes all in one satisfying, glowing piece; others, by

   patching together little bits of it, manage to salvage enough to keep warm.

b. America has been called a country of pragmatists; although the American

   devotion to ideals is legendary.

c. The first requirement is honesty, everything else follows.

d. I am not fond of opera, I must admit; however, that I was greatly moved by

   Les Misérables.

e. Delegates to the convention came from Basel, Switzerland, Waikiki, Hawaii,

   Nome, Alaska, and Pretoria, South Africa.

1. When she entered the room, everyone quit discussing the incident; until she

   had finished her errand and left.

2. Martin Luther King, Jr., who forged the nonviolent civil rights movement in the United States, had not intended to be a preacher; initially, he had planned to become a lawyer.

3. Severe, unremitting pain is a ravaging force; especially when the patient tries to hide it from others.

4. I entered this class feeling jittery and incapable, I leave feeling poised and confident.

5. Our physical education teacher always matched the punishment to the crime, for example, for talking during class, I had to write a five-hundred-word essay entitled "The Glories of Silence."

EXERCISE P4-1 The colon, the semicolon, and the comma
If you have problems with this exercise, see pp. 158–62 in
A Writer's Reference, Second Edition.

Edit the following sentences to correct errors in the use of the comma, the semi-colon, or the colon. If a sentence is correct, write "correct" after it. Answers to lettered sentences appear in the back of the booklet. Example:

Smiling confidently, the young man stated his major goal in life : to
be secretary of agriculture before he was thirty.

a. The second and most memorable week of survival school consisted of five stages: orientation; long treks; POW camp; escape and evasion; and return to civilization.

b. Among the canceled classes were: calculus, physics, advanced biology, and English 101.

c. His only desires were for vengeance; vengeance for his father's death, vengeance for his mother's loss of eyesight, vengeance for his own lost youth.

d. For example: when a student in private school is caught with drugs, he or she is immediately expelled.

e. In the introduction to his wife's book on gardening, E.B. White describes her writing process: "The editor in her fought the writer every inch of the way; the struggle was felt all through the house. She would write eight or ten words, then draw her gun and shoot them down."

1. The patient survived for one reason, the medics got to her in time.

2. While traveling through France, Helen visited: the Loire Valley, Chartres, the Louvre, and the McDonald's stand at the foot of the Eiffel Tower.

3. I'm from Missouri you must show me.

4. Historian Robert Kee looks to the past for the source of the political troubles in Ireland: "If blame is to be apportioned for today's situation in Northern Ireland, it should be laid not at the door of men today but of history."

5. Dean Summerfelt had several projects to complete before leaving for vacation; hiring a data-processing instructor, completing a report on curriculum revision, and defending the departmental budget at the annual budget hearing.

Edit the following sentences to correct errors in the use of the apostrophe. If a sentence is correct, write "correct" after it. Answers to lettered sentences appear in the back of the booklet. Example:

Marietta lived above the only bar in town, Smiling ~~Jacks.~~ Jack's.

a. In a democracy anyones vote counts as much as mine.

b. He received two A's, three B's, and a C.

c. The puppy's favorite activity was chasing it's tail.

d. After we bought J.J. the latest style pants and shirts, he decided that last years faded, ragged jeans were perfect for all occasions.

e. A crocodiles' life span is about thirteen years.

1. The snow doesn't rise any higher than the horses' fetlocks. [*more than one horse*]

2. For a bus driver, complaints, fare disputes, and robberies are all part of a days work.

3. Each day the menu features a different European countries' dish.

4. We cleared four years accumulation of trash out of the attic; its amazing how much junk can pile up.

5. Booties are placed on the sled dogs feet to protect them from sharp rocks and ice. [*more than one dog*]

6. Sue and Ann went to a party for a friend of theirs'.

7. Three teenage son's can devour about as much food as four full-grown field hands. The only difference is that they dont do half as much work.

8. Ethiopians's meals were served on fermented bread.

9. Luck is an important element in a rock musicians career.

10. My sister-in-law's quilts are being shown at the Fendrick Gallery.

EXERCISE P6-1   Quotation marks   If you have problems with this exercise, see pp. 165–70 in *A Writer's Reference,* Second Edition.

Add or delete quotation marks as needed and make any other necessary changes in punctuation in the following sentences. If a sentence is correct, write "correct" after it. Answers to lettered sentences appear in the back of the booklet. Example:

Bill Cosby once said, "I don't know the key to success, but the key to failure is trying to please everyone."

a. Fire and Ice is one of Robert Frost's most famous poems.

b. As Emerson wrote in 1849, I hate quotations. Tell me what you know.

c. Joggers have to run up the hills and then back down, but bicyclers, once they reach the top of a hill, get a "free ride" back down.

d. "Ladies and gentlemen," said the emcee, "I am happy to present our guest speaker.

e. Historians Segal and Stineback tell us that the English settlers considered these epidemics "the hand of God making room for His followers in the "New World"."

1. The dispatcher's voice cut through the still night air: "Scout 41, robbery in progress, alley rear of 58th and Blaine.

2. For the body to turn sugar into glucose, other nutrients in the body must be used. Sugar "steals" these other nutrients from the body.

3. Kara looked hopelessly around the small locked room. "If only I were a flea," she thought, "I could get out of here."

4. My skiing instructor promised us that "we would all be ready for the intermediate slope in one week."

5. After the movie Vicki said, "The reviewer called this flick "trash of the first order." I guess you can't believe everything you read."

6. Some critics believe that when Hamlet says "To be, or not to be, that is the question," he knows that others are hidden in the room watching him.

7. Who said, "I have sworn upon the altar of God eternal hostility against every form of tyranny"?

8. As David Anable has written: "The time is approaching when we will be able to select the news we want to read from a pocket computer."

9. "Could one define the word 'red,' asks Wittgenstein, "by pointing to something that was *not red?*"

10. One of my favorite poems is Langston Hughes's 'Mother to Son.'

EXERCISE P7-1 The period, the question mark, and the exclamation point If you have problems with this exercise, see pp. 171–73 in *A Writer's Reference*, Second Edition.

Add appropriate end punctuation in the following paragraph.

Although I am generally rational, I am superstitious I never walk under
ladders or put shoes on the table If I spill the salt, I go into frenzied calisthenics
picking up the grains and tossing them over my left shoulder As a result of these
curious activities, I've always wondered whether • knowing the roots of superstitions
would quell my irrational responses Superstition has it, for example, that one
should never place a hat on the bed This superstition arises from a time when head
lice where quite common and placing a guest's hat on the bed stood a good chance of
spreading lice through the host's bed Doesn't this make good sense And doesn't it
stand to reason that if I know that my guests don't have lice I shouldn't care where
their hats go Of course it does It is fair to ask, then, whether I have changed my
ways and place hats on beds Are you kidding I wouldn't put a hat on a bed if my life
depended on it

EXERCISE P7-2   Other punctuation marks   If you have
problems with this exercise, see pp. 173–76 in *A Writer's Reference,*
Second Edition.

Edit the following sentences for punctuation problems, focusing especially on appropriate use of the dash, parentheses, brackets, ellipsis mark, and slash. If a sentence is correct, write "correct" after it. Answers to lettered sentences appear in the
back of the booklet. Example:

> **Social insects/¬bees, for example/¬are able to communicate quite
> complicated messages to their fellows.**

a. We lived in Iowa (Davenport, to be specific) during the early years of our

    marriage.

b. Every night — after her jazzercise class — Elizabeth bragged about how

    invigorated she felt, but she always looked exhausted.

---

c. *Infoworld* reports that "customers without any particular aptitude for computers can easily learn to use it [the Bay Area Teleguide] through simple, three-step instructions located at the booth."

d. Cancer — a disease that strikes without regard to age, race, or religion and causes dread in the most stalwart person, had struck my family.

e. The class stood, faced the flag, placed hands over hearts, and raced through "I pledge allegiance — liberty and justice for all" in less than sixty seconds.

1. Of the three basic schools of detective fiction, the tea-and-crumpet, the hardboiled detective, and the police procedural, I find the quaint, civilized quality of the tea-and-crumpet school the most appealing.

2. In *Lifeboat,* Alfred Hitchcock appears (some say without his knowledge) in a newspaper advertisement for weight loss.

3. There are three points of etiquette in poker: 1, always allow someone to cut the cards, 2. don't forget to ante up, and 3. never stack your chips.

4. "April is the cruelest month . . . ," wrote T. S. Eliot, but we all know that February holds that honor.

5. The old Valentine verse we used to chant said it all: "Roses are red, / violets are blue, / sugar is sweet, / and so are you."

Punctuate the following letter.

27 Latches Lane

Missoula Missouri 55432

April 16 1992

Dear Rosalie

I have to tell you about the accident We were driving home at around 5 30 PM of course wed be on the Schuylkill Expressway at rush hour when a tan Cutlass smashed us in the rear Luckily we all had our seatbelts fastened Dr. Schabbles who was in the back seat and my husband Bob complained of whiplash but really we got off with hardly a scratch

The mother and daughter in the Cutlass however werent as fortunate They ended up with surgical collars and Ace bandages but their car certainly fared better than ours

The driver of the third car involved in the accident confused everyone Although her car was in the front of the line she kept saying I hit the tan car I hit the tan car We didnt understand until she told us that a fourth car had hit her in the rear and had pushed her ahead of all the rest Can you imagine how frustrated we were when we found out that this man the one who had started it all had left the scene of the accident You were the last car in line someone said No you were we answered The policeman had to reconstruct the disaster from the hopeless babble of eight witnesses

Its uncanny Out of 34800 cars on the expressway on April 14 the police keep count you know our car had to be the one in front of that monstrous tan Cutlass

Well I just wanted to send you a report I hope your days are less thrilling than mine

Yours

Marie

MECHANICS

EXERCISE M1-1 Capital letters   If you have problems with this exercise, see pp. 179–82 in *A Writer's Reference,* Second Edition.

Edit the following sentences to correct errors in capitalization. If a sentence is correct, write "correct" after it. Answers to lettered sentences appear in the back of the booklet. Example:

> On our trip to the West we visited the *G*rand *C*anyon and the *G*reat *S*alt *D*esert.

a. District attorney Johnson was disgusted when the jurors turned in a verdict of not guilty after only one hour of deliberation.

b. My mother has begun to research the history of her indian ancestors in North Carolina.

c. W. C. Fields's epitaph reads, "On the whole, I'd rather be in Philadelphia."

d. Refugees from central America are finding it more and more difficult to cross the rio Grande into the United States.

e. I want to take Environmental Biology 103, one other Biology course, and one English course.

1. "Forbidding people things they like or think they might enjoy," contends Gore Vidal, "Only makes them want those things all the more."

2. If someone were to approach me looking for the secret to running a good bar, I suppose I'd offer the following advice: Get your customers to pour out their ideas at a greater rate than you pour out the liquor.

3. Does your Aunt still preach in local churches whenever she's asked?

4. Historians have described Robert E. Lee as the aristocratic south personified.

5. My brother is a Doctor and my sister-in-law is an Attorney.

EXERCISE M2-1 Abbreviations If you have problems with this exercise, see pp. 182–85 in *A Writer's Reference,* Second Edition.

Edit the following sentences to correct errors in abbreviations. If a sentence is correct, write "correct" after it. Answers to lettered sentences appear in the back of the booklet. Example:

> This year ~~Xmas~~ *Christmas* will fall on a ~~Fri.~~ *Friday.*

a. Marlon Mansard, a reporter for CBS, received a congressional citation for his work in Lebanon.

b. My grandmother told me that of all the subjects she studied, she found econ. the most challenging.

c. The Rev. Martin Luther King, Sr., spoke eloquently about his son's work against segregation in the South.

d. The first discovery of America was definitely not in 1492 A.D.

e. Turning to p. 195, Marion realized that she had finally reached the end of ch. 22.

1. Many girls fall prey to a cult worship of great entertainers — e.g., in my generation, girls worshiped the Beatles.

2. Three interns were selected to assist the chief surgeon, Dr. Paul Hunter, M.D., in the hospital's first heart-lung transplant.

3. Some historians think that the New Testament was completed by A.D. 100.

4. My soc. prof. spends most of his lecture time talking about political science.

5. Distinctions between the CIA and the FBI may not seem important, but they are.

EXERCISE M3-1 Numbers If you have problems with this exercise, see pp. 185–86 in *A Writer's Reference,* Second Edition.

Edit the following sentences to correct errors in the use of numbers. If a sentence is correct, write "correct" after it. Answers to lettered sentences appear in the back of the booklet. Example:

By the end of the evening Brandon had only ~~three dollars and six cents~~ **left.** $3.06

a. We have ordered 4 azaleas, 3 rhododendrons, and 2 mountain laurels for the back area of the garden.

b. The president of Vivelle Cotton announced that all shifts would report back to work at the Augusta plant on June 6, 1990.

c. The score was tied at 5–5 when the momentum shifted and carried the Standards to a decisive 12–5 win.

d. We ordered three four-door sedans for company executives.

e. In nineteen eighty-nine, only one hundred and two male high school students in our state planned to make a career of teaching.

1. One of my favorite scenes in Shakespeare is the property division scene in Act I of *King Lear.*

2. The president's plane will arrive in Houston at 6:30 P.M.

3. 90 of the firm's employees signed up for the insurance program.

4. After her 5th marriage ended in divorce, Melinda decided to give up her quest for the perfect husband.

5. With 6 students and 2 teachers, the class had a 3:1 student-teacher ratio.

EXERCISE M4-1   Italics (underlining)   If you have problems with this exercise, see pp. 187–88 in *A Writer's Reference,* Second Edition.

Edit the following sentences to correct errors in the use of italics. If a sentence is correct, write "correct" after it. Answers to lettered sentences appear in the back of the booklet. Example:

> Leaves of Grass by Walt Whitman was quite controversial when it was published a century ago.

a. Howard Hughes commissioned the Spruce Goose, a beautifully built but thoroughly impractical wooden aircraft.

b. Pulaski was so *exhausted* he could barely lift his foot the six inches to the elevator floor.

c. Even though it is almost always hot in Mexico in the summer, you can usually find a cool spot on one of the park benches in the town's zócalo.

---

d. I will never forget the way he whispered the word *finished.*

e. One of my favorite novels is George Eliot's "Middlemarch."

1. Bernard watched as Eileen stood transfixed in front of Vermeer's Head of a Young Girl.

2. The preacher was partial to quotations from Exodus.

3. I learned the Latin term ad infinitum from an old nursery rhyme about fleas: "Great fleas have little fleas upon their back to bite 'em. / Little fleas have lesser fleas and so on ad infinitum."

4. Redford and Newman in the movie "The Sting" were amateurs compared with the seventeen-year-old con artist who lives at our house.

5. I find it impossible to remember the second *l* in *llama.*

EXERCISE M5-1 Spelling If you have problems with this exercise, see pp. 189–93 in *A Writer's Reference,* Second Edition.

Ask a friend or classmate to dictate the following paragraph to you. When you have transcribed it, check your version with this one. Note any words that you misspelled and practice writing them correctly.

The members of a faculty committee that recommends changes in course requirements invited several students to meet with them. In their invitation, the members emphasized that even though they would ask specific questions, they especially wanted the students to discuss their experience in various courses and to offer suggestions for changes. The students who were chosen represented a variety of academic interests, and the committee particularly selected students who were in their first year and in their last year. In his separate interview with

---

with the committee, John, who is graduating in May, questioned whether it was necessary to take so many courses that were apparently unrelated to his business major. He acknowledged that the requirement for some courses outside his major was legitimate; however, he believed that more thorough preparation for his specialty, international finance, would have been appropriate. John was worried because the job market had become so competitive, and he did not feel that he had benefited from some of the courses he had taken outside the business school. John apologized for being so negative, and he praised the committee for its willingness to listen to the opinions of students.

EXERCISE M5-2 Spelling   If you have problems with this exercise, see pp. 189–93 in *A Writer's Reference,* Second Edition.

The following paragraphs have been run through a spell checker on a computer. Proofread them carefully, editing the spelling and typographical errors that remain.

Later, John wrote a letter to the faculty committee, describing the kinds of classes that had had the greatest affect on him. John's letter impressed the committee, because he was able to site specific professors and specific teaching method. He started his letter very candidly: "Even though your professors, I must say that the best learning experiences I had did not involve the professor, accept as a resource or as a guide." John explained that he achieved more when he was actively involved in the class then when he sat and listened to the professor lecturing and asking questions.

John praised one professor in particular, an imminent psychologist and author. "When Professor Howell past control to the class," wrote John, "we took this as a complement. We had all assumed that being subjected to lengthy, boring lectures was a fundamental principal in higher education, but Professor Howell proved us wrong." In his letter, John went one to describe how the class was taught. Professor Howell asked each student to give reports, and she regularly had small groups discuss material or solve specific problems and report to the class. She participated in the class, to, but students had more access to her as she circulated though the room to answer questions or to challenge students to think in different ways. John closed his letter with further praise for Professor Howell and for teachers like her, saying, "Their what I'll remember most about my educational experiences in college."

EXERCISE M6-1 The hyphen If you have problems with this exercise, see pp. 194–96 in *A Writer's Reference,* Second Edition.

Edit the following sentences to correct errors in hyphenation. If a sentence is correct, write "correct" after it. Answers to lettered sentences appear in the back of the booklet. Example:

Zola's first readers were scandalized by his slice–of–life novels.
$\wedge \quad \wedge$

a. Gold is the seventy-ninth element in the periodic table.

b. The quietly-purring cat cleaned first one paw and then the other before curling up under the stove.

c. Many states are adopting laws that limit pro-
    perty taxes for homeowners.

d. Your dog is well-known in our neighborhood.

e. He did fifty push-ups in two minutes and then collapsed.

1. We knew we were driving too fast when our tires skidded over the rain slick surface.

---

2. Many people protested when the drinking age was lowered from twenty-one to twenty.

3. Instead of an old Victorian, we settled for a modern split-level surrounded by maples.

4. One-quarter of the class signed up for the debate on U.S. foreign aid to Latin America.

5. At the end of *Macbeth*, the hero feels himself profoundly alone.

BASIC GRAMMAR

EXERCISE B1-1   Parts of speech: nouns   If you have problems with this exercise, see p. 265 in *A Writer's Reference, Second Edition.*

Underline the nouns (and nouns functioning as adjectives) in the following sentences. Answers to lettered sentences appear in the back of the booklet. Example:

<u>Pride</u> is at the <u>bottom</u> of all great <u>mistakes.</u>

a. Clothe an idea in words, and it loses its freedom of movement.

b. Idle hands are the devil's workshop.

c. Our national flower is the concrete cloverleaf.

d. The ultimate censorship is the flick of the dial.

e. Figures won't lie, but liars will figure.

1. Conservatism is the worship of dead revolutions.

2. The winds and the waves are always on the side of the ablest navigators.

3. Problems are opportunities in work clothes.

4. A scalded dog fears even cold water.

5. Prejudice is the child of ignorance.

EXERCISE B1-2   Parts of speech: pronouns   If you have
problems with this exercise, see pp. 265–67 in *A Writer's Reference,*
Second Edition.

Underline the pronouns (and pronouns functioning as adjectives) in the following
sentences. Answers to lettered sentences appear in the back of the booklet. Example:

Beware of persons <u>who</u> are praised by <u>everyone</u>.

a. Every society honors its live conformists and its dead troublemakers.

b. Watch the faces of those who bow low.

c. I have written some poetry that I myself don't understand.

d. A skeptic is a person who would ask God for his I.D.

e. No one can be hanged for thinking.

1. Doctors can bury their mistakes, but architects can only advise their clients
   to plant vines.

2. Nothing is interesting if you are not interested.

3. We will never have friends if we expect to find them without fault.

4. If a man bites a dog, that is news.

5. Anyone who serves God for money will serve the devil for better wages.

If you have problems
with this exercise, see pp. 267–68 in *A Writer's Reference*, Second
Edition.

Underline the verbs in the following sentences, including helping verbs and parti-
cles. Answers to lettered sentences appear in the back of the booklet. Example:

> **<u>Throw</u> a lucky man into the sea, and he <u>will emerge</u> with a fish in his
> mouth.**

a. Great persons have not commonly been great scholars.

b. Without the spice of guilt, can sin be fully savored?

c. One arrow does not bring down two birds.

d. Birds of a feather flock together.

e. Don't scald your tongue in other people's broth.

1. The king can do no wrong.

2. The road to ruin is always kept in good repair.

3. Love your neighbor, but don't pull down the hedge.

4. Life can only be understood backward, but it must be lived forward.

5. He has every attribute of a dog except loyalty.

Parts of speech: adjectives and adverbs If you have problems with this exercise, see pp. 268–69 in *A Writer's Reference,* Second Edition.

Underline the adjectives and circle the adverbs in the following sentences. If a word is a pronoun in form but an adjective in function, treat it as an adjective. Also, treat the articles *a, an,* and *the* as adjectives. Answers to lettered sentences appear in the back of the booklet. Example:

> A little sincerity is a dangerous thing, and a great deal of it is
>
> (absolutely) fatal.

a. Little strokes fell great oaks.

b. The American public is wonderfully tolerant.

c. You cannot spoil a rotten egg.

d. Hope is a very thin diet.

e. Sleep faster. We need the pillows.

1. We cannot be too careful in the choice of our enemies.

2. A clean glove often hides a dirty hand.

3. Money will buy a pretty good dog, but it will not buy the wag of its tail.

4. Loquacious people seldom have much sense.

5. An old quarrel can be easily revived.

EXERCISE B2-1   **Parts of sentences: subjects**   If you have
problems with this exercise, see pp. 271–72 in *A Writer's Reference,*
Second Edition.

In the following sentences, underline the complete subject and write *ss* above the
simple subject(s). If the subject is an understood *you,* insert it in parentheses. Answers to lettered sentences appear in the back of the booklet. Example:

               ss
   <u>A little inaccuracy</u> sometimes saves many explanations.

a. A spoiled child never loves its mother.

b. To some lawyers, all facts are created equal.

c. Speak softly and carry a big stick.

d. There is nothing permanent except change.

e. Does hope really spring eternal in the human breast?

1. Habit is overcome by habit.

2. The gardens of kindness never fade.

3. The dog with the bone is always in danger.

4. Fools and their money are soon parted.

5. There is honor among thieves.

EXERCISE B2-2   Parts of sentences: objects and comple-
ments   If you have problems with this exercise, see pp. 272–74
in *A Writer's Reference,* Second Edition.

Label the subject complements, direct objects, indirect objects, and object complements in the following sentences. If an object or complement consists of more than
one word, bracket and label all of it. Answers to lettered sentences appear in the
back of the booklet. Example:

$$\overset{DO}{} \quad \overset{OC}{}$$

All work and no play make Jack a dull boy.

a.   Victory has a hundred fathers, but defeat is an orphan.

b.   No one tests the depth of a river with both feet.

c.   Lock your door and keep your neighbors honest.

d.   Not every day can be a feast of lanterns.

e.   Lizzie Borden gave her father forty whacks.

1.   Good medicine always tastes bitter.

2.   Ask me no questions, and I will tell you no lies.

3.   The mob has many heads but no brains.

4.   Some folk want their luck buttered.

5.   Prejudice is the child of ignorance.

EXERCISE B3-1 Subordinate word groups: prepositional phrases
If you have problems with this exercise, see p. 274 in *A Writer's Reference,* Second Edition.

Underline the prepositional phrases in the following sentences. Be prepared to explain the function of each phrase. Answers to lettered sentences appear in the back of the booklet. Example:

> **You can tell the ideals <u>of a nation</u> <u>by its advertising</u>.**
> [Adjective phrase modifying <u>ideals</u>; adverbial phrase modifying <u>can tell</u>.]

a. Laughter is a tranquilizer with no side effects.

b. One misfortune always carries another on its back.

c. The love of money is the root of all evil.

d. Wall Street begins in a graveyard and ends in a river.

e. You can stroke people with words.

1. A pleasant companion reduces the length of the journey.

2. A society of sheep produces a government of wolves.

3. Some people feel with their heads and think with their hearts.

4. In love and war, all is fair.

5. He leaped from the frying pan into the fire.

EXERCISE B3-2   Subordinate word groups: verbal phrases

If you have problems with this exercise, see p. 275 in *A Writer's Reference*, Second Edition.

Underline the verbal phrases in the following sentences. Be prepared to explain the function of each phrase. Answers to lettered sentences appear in the back of the booklet. Example:

> **Fate tried <u>to conceal him</u> by <u>naming him Smith</u>.** [Infinitive phrase used as direct object; gerund phrase used as object of the preposition *by*.]

a. The best substitute for experience is being sixteen.

b. Concealing a disease is no way to cure it.

c. To help a friend is to give ourselves pleasure.

d. Beware of Greeks bearing gifts.

e. Every genius is considerably helped by being dead.

1. The thing generally raised on city land is taxes.

2. Do not use a hatchet to remove a fly from your friend's forehead.

3. He has the gall of a shoplifter returning an item for a refund.

4. Do you want to be a writer? Then write.

5. Being weak, foxes are distinguished by superior tact.

EXERCISE B3-3 Subordinate word groups: subordinate
clauses   If you have problems with this exercise, see pp. 276–77
in *A Writer's Reference,* Second Edition.

Underline the subordinate clauses in the following sentences. Be prepared to explain the function of each clause. Answers to lettered sentences appear in the back of the booklet. Example:

When the insects take over the world, we hope that they will
remember our picnics with gratitude.   [Adverb clause modifying
hope; noun clause used as direct object.]

a. Though you live near a forest, do not waste firewood.

b. The gods help those who help themselves.

c. What is written without effort is read without pleasure.

d. The dog that trots finds the bone.

e. A fraud is not perfect unless it is practiced on clever persons.

1. What history teaches us is that we have never learned anything from it.

2. Dig a well before you are thirsty.

3. Whoever named it necking was a poor judge of anatomy.

4. If you were born lucky, even your rooster will lay eggs.

5. He gave her a look that you could have poured on a waffle.

EXERCISE B4-1 Sentence types If you have problems with this exercise, see pp. 277–78 in *A Writer's Reference,* Second Edition.

Identify the following sentences as simple, compound, complex, or compound-complex. Be prepared to identify the subordinate clauses and classify them according to their function: adjective, adverb, or noun. Answers to lettered sentences appear in the back of the booklet. Example:

> **My folks didn't come over on the Mayflower; they were there to meet the boat.** *compound*

a. The poet is a liar who always speaks the truth.

b. Before marriage, keep your eyes wide open; afterward, keep them half shut.

c. The frog in the well knows nothing of the ocean.

d. If you don't go to other people's funerals, they won't go to yours.

e. People who sleep like a baby usually don't have one.

1. We often give our enemies the means for our own destruction.

2. Those who write clearly have readers; those who write obscurely have commentators.

3. The impersonal hand of government can never replace the helping hand of a neighbor.

4. Human action can be modified to some extent, but human nature cannot be changed.

5. When an elephant is in trouble, even a frog will kick him.

Answers to Lettered Exercises

EFFECTIVE SENTENCES

EXERCISE E1-1 Parallelism page 1

Possible revisions:
  a. The system has capabilities such as communicating with other computers, processing records, and performing mathematical functions.
  b. The personnel officer told me that I would answer the phone, welcome visitors, distribute mail, and do some typing.
  c. This summer I want a job more than a trip to Disney World.
  d. Mary told the judge that she had been pulled out of a line of fast-moving traffic and that she had a perfect driving record.
  e. Nancy not only called the post office but checked with the neighbors to see if the package had come.

EXERCISE E2-1 Needed words page 2

Possible revisions:
  a. Carmen believed that all four politicians on the talk show were lying.
  b. Some say that Ella Fitzgerald's renditions of Cole Porter's songs are better than any other singer's.
  c. SETI (the Search for Extraterrestrial Intelligence) has excited and will continue to excite interest among space buffs.
  d. Samantha got along better with the chimpanzees than with Albert. [*or* ... than Albert did.]
  e. Myra was both interested in and concerned about her father's will.

EXERCISE E3-1 Misplaced modifiers page 4

Possible revisions:
  a. He wanted to buy only three roses, not a dozen.
  b. Within the next few years, orthodontists will be using Kurtz's technique as standard practice.
  c. Celia received a flier from a Japanese nun about a workshop on making a kimono.
  d. The media falsely accused the Secret Service of mishandling the attempted assassination.
  e. Each state would set into motion a program of recycling all reusable products.

Answers to Lettered Exercises   **91**

EXERCISE E3-2 Dangling modifiers *page 5*

Possible revisions:

a. Reaching the heart, the surgeon performed a bypass on the severely blocked arteries.
b. As I nestled in the cockpit, the pounding of the engine was muffled only slightly by my helmet.
c. Feeling unprepared for the exam, June found the questions as hard as her instructor had suggested they would be.
d. While my sister was still a beginner at tennis, the coaches recruited her to train for the Olympics.
e. To protest the arms buildup, demonstrators set bonfires throughout the park.

EXERCISE E4-1 Shifts *page 6*

Possible revisions:

a. We waited in the emergency room for about an hour. Finally, the nurse came in and told us that we were in the wrong place.
b. Newspapers put the lurid details of an armed robbery on page 1 and relegate the warm, human-interest stories to page G-10.
c. Ministers often have a hard time because they have to please so many different people.
d. We drove for eight hours until we reached the South Dakota Badlands. We could hardly believe the eeriness of the landscape at dusk.
e. The question is whether ferrets bred in captivity have the instinct to prey on prairie dogs or whether this is a learned skill.

EXERCISE E5-1 Mixed constructions *page 7*

Possible revisions:

a. My instant reaction was anger and disappointment.
b. I brought a problem into the house that my mother wasn't sure how to handle.
c. It is through the misery of others that old Harvey has become rich.
d. A cloverleaf allows traffic on limited-access freeways to change direction.
e. Bowman established the format that future football card companies would emulate for years to come.

EXERCISE E6-2 Coordination and subordination *page 10*

Possible revisions:

a. After a couple of minutes, the teacher walked in smiling.
b. The losing team was made up of superstars who acted as isolated individuals on the court.
c. Because we are concerned about the environment, we keep our use of insecticides, herbicides, and fungicides to a minimum.
d. The aides help the younger children with reading and math, their weakest subjects.
e. My first sky dive, from an altitude of 12,500 feet, was the most frightening experience of my life.

EXERCISE E6-3 Faulty subordination *page 11*

Possible revisions:

a. When our team finally acquired an expert backstroker, we won every relay for the rest of the season.
b. The senator's planned trip to Spain and Portugal was canceled because of terrorist activities.
c. When I presented the idea of job sharing to my supervisors, to my surprise they were delighted with the idea.
d. Although outsiders have forced changes on them, native Hawaiians try to preserve their ancestors' sacred customs.
e. Sharon's country kitchen, formerly a lean-to porch, overlooks a field where horses and cattle graze among old tombstones.

WORD CHOICE

EXERCISE W1-1 Usage *page 14*

Possible revisions:

a. The number of horses a Comanche warrior had in his possession indicated the wealth of his family.
b. The cat just sat there watching his prey.
c. We will telephone you as soon as the tickets arrive.
d. Changing attitudes toward alcohol have affected the beer industry.
e. Chris redesigned the boundary plantings to try to improve the garden's overall design.

EXERCISE W2-1 Wordy sentences *page 15*

Possible revisions:

a. When visitors come, Grandmother just stares at the wall.
b. Dr. Sandford has seen problems like yours many times.
c. Bloom's race for the governorship is futile.
d. New fares must be reported to all of our transportation offices.
e. In Biology 10A a faculty tutor will assign you eight taped modules and clarify any information on the tapes.

EXERCISE W3-1 Jargon and pretentious language *page 17*

Possible revisions:

a. It is a widely held myth that middle-aged people can't change.
b. Have you ever been accused of beating a dead horse?
c. I crawled on my elbows about ten yards to the trench.
d. When our father was laid off from his high-paying factory job, we learned what it was like to be poor.
e. If you cannot install the computer, you may call the firm's 800 number to get help.

EXERCISE W3-3   Sexist language   *page 19*

Possible revisions:
  a. Harriet Glover is the defense attorney appointed by the court. Al Jones has been assigned to work with her on the case.
  b. A young graduate who is careful about investments can accumulate a significant sum in a relatively short period.
  c. An elementary school teacher should understand the concept of nurturing if he or she intends to be a success.
  d. Because Dr. Brown and Dr. Coombs were the senior professors in the department, they served as co-chairpersons of the promotion committee.
  e. If we do not stop polluting our environment, we will perish.

EXERCISE W4-1   Active verbs   *page 20*

Possible revisions:
  a. The processor automatically develops, fixes, washes, and dries the film.
  b. The producer overlooks the entire operation.
  c. Active
  d. Escaping into the world of drugs, I rebelled against anything and everything laid down by the establishment.
  e. Players were fighting on both sides of the rink.

EXERCISE W4-2   Misused words   *page 22*

Possible revisions:
  a. Many of us are not persistent enough to make a change for the better.
  b. Mrs. Altman's comments were meant to evoke [*or* provoke] a response from the class.
  c. Sam Brown began his career as a lawyer, but now he is a real estate mogul.
  d. When Robert Frost died at age eighty-eight, he left a legacy of poems that will make him immortal.
  e. This patient is kept in isolation to prevent her from catching our germs.

EXERCISE W4-3   Standard idioms   *page 23*

  a. I was so angry with the salesperson that I took her bag of samples and emptied it on the floor in front of her.
  b. Correct
  c. Try to come up with the rough outline, and we will find someone who can fill in the details.
  d. "Your prejudice is no different from mine," she shouted.
  e. The parade moved off the street and onto the beach.

EXERCISE W4-4   Clichés and mixed figures of speech   *page 24*

Possible revisions:
  a. His fellow club members deliberated very briefly; all agreed that his behavior was unacceptable.
  b. The president thought that the scientists were using science as a means of furthering their political goals.

c. Architect I.M. Pei gave our city a new cultural spirit that led to a renaissance.
d. We ironed out the wrinkles in our relationship.
e. Mel told us that he wasn't willing to take the chance.

GRAMMATICAL SENTENCES

EXERCISE G1-1 Subject-verb agreement   *page 25*

a. Subject: friendship and support; verb: have; b. Subject: rings; verb: are; c. Subject: Each; verb: has; d. Subject: source; verb: is; e. Subject: windows; verb: were

EXERCISE G1-2 Subject-verb agreement   *page 26*

a. High concentrations of carbon monoxide result in headaches, dizziness, unconsciousness, and even death.
b. Correct
c. Correct
d. Crystal chandeliers, polished floors, and a new oil painting have transformed Sandra's apartment.
e. Either Alice or Jan usually works the midnight shift.

EXERCISE G2-1 Irregular verbs   *page 29*

a. Noticing that my roommate was shivering and looking pale, I rang for the nurse.
b. When I get the urge to exercise, I lie down until it passes.
c. Correct
d. The team of engineers watched in horror as the newly built dam burst and flooded the small valley.
e. Correct

EXERCISE G2-2 -s and -ed verb forms and omitted verbs   *page 30*

a. Correct
b. The police are used to helping lost tourists.
c. The whooping crane has been an endangered species since the late 1930s.
d. We often don't know whether he is angry or just joking.
e. Staggered working hours have reduced traffic jams and saved motorists many gallons of gas.

EXERCISE G2-3 Verb tense and mood   *page 31*

a. Correct
b. Watson and Crick discovered the mechanism that controls inheritance in all life: the workings of the DNA molecule.
c. Marion would write more if she weren't distracted by a house full of children.
d. Sharon told me that she had gone to the meeting the day before.
e. Correct.

EXERCISE G3-1   Pronoun-antecedent agreement   *page 34*

Possible revisions:
- a. All students who are taking the school bus to the volleyball game must bring in a permission slip signed by their parents.
- b. Correct
- c. Late at night, I sometimes saw a priest or a brother entering the side door of the church, his face silhouetted briefly in the moonlight.
- d. A climatologist collects weather data from around the world, analyzes the data, and then passes the analyses along to forecasters.
- e. If you have any students attending class who are still not on your roster, please send them to the registration office.

EXERCISE G3-3   Pronoun reference   *page 36*

Possible revisions:
- a. The detective photographed the body after removing the blood-stained shawl.
- b. In Professor Johnson's class, students are lucky to earn a C.
- c. Satanism is a serious problem in our country. Its rites are grotesque perversions of many of Christianity's sacred rituals.
- d. The Comanche braves lived violent lives; they gained respect for their skill as warriors.
- e. All students can secure parking permits from the campus police office, which is open from 8 A.M. until 8 P.M.

EXERCISE G3-4   Pronoun case: personal
pronouns   *page 38*

- a. My Ethiopian neighbor was puzzled by the dedication of us joggers.
- b. Correct
- c. Sue's husband is ten years older than she.
- d. The winners, Julie and he, were unable to attend the awards ceremony.
- e. The chances against your getting hit by lightning are about two million to one.

EXERCISE G3-5   Pronoun case: *who* and *whom*   *page 39*

- a. In his first production of *Hamlet,* whom did Laurence Olivier replace?
- b. Correct
- c. Correct
- d. Some group leaders cannot handle the pressure; they give whoever makes the most noise most of their attention.
- e. One of the women whom Johnson hired became the most successful lawyer in the agency.

EXERCISE G4-1   Adjectives and adverbs   *page 41*

- a. My mechanic showed me exactly where to wrap the wire firmly around the muffler.
- b. All of us on the team felt bad about our performance.
- c. My mother thinks that Carmen is the more pleasant of the twins.
- d. Correct
- e. Last Christmas was the most wonderful day of my life.

EXERCISE G5-1 Sentence fragments *page 43*

Possible revisions:

   a. As I stood in front of the microwave, I recalled my grandmother bending over her old black stove and remembered what she taught me: that any food can have soul if you love the people you are cooking for.
   b. It has been said that there are only three indigenous American art forms: jazz, musical comedy, and soap opera.
   c. Correct
   d. Myra did not tell us about her new job for six weeks, although she saw one or the other of us every day.
   e. While on a tour of Italy, Maria and Kathleen sneaked away from their group to spend some quiet minutes with Leonardo da Vinci's *Last Supper,* a stunning fresco painted in the fifteenth century in a Milan monastery.

EXERCISE G6-1 Comma splices and fused sentences *page 45*

Possible revisions:

   a. The city had one public swimming pool that stayed packed with children all summer long.
   b. Most parents want their children to do well in school, but they don't always know how to help them succeed.
   c. Why should we pay taxes to support public transportation? We prefer to save energy dollars by carpooling.
   d. Suddenly there was a loud silence; the shelling had stopped.
   e. As I walked into the living room, a special report flashed onto the TV screen: The space shuttle had exploded.

EXERCISE G6-2 Comma splices and fused sentences *page 47*

Possible revisions:

   a. Because the trail up Mount Finegold was declared impassable, we decided to return to our hotel a day early.
   b. Correct
   c. The officer must enforce the laws, even when the laws seem unfair.
   d. Researchers studying the fertility of Texas land tortoises X-rayed all the female tortoises to see how many eggs they had.
   e. The suburbs seemed cold; they lacked the warmth and excitement of our Italian neighborhood.

ESL TROUBLE SPOTS

EXERCISE T2-1 Helping verbs and main verbs *page 51*

   a. We will make this a better country.
   b. There is nothing in the world that TV has not touched on.
   c. Did you understand my question?
   d. A hard wind was blowing while we were climbing the mountain.
   e. The child's innocent world has been taken away from him.

EXERCISE T2-2 Verbs in conditional sentences *page 52*

Possible revisions:
a. If I had had the money, I would have met my friends in Barcelona last summer.
b. If Martin Luther King, Jr., were alive today, he would be appalled by the violence in our inner cities.
c. Whenever my uncle comes to visit, he brings me an expensive gift.
d. We will lose our largest client unless we update our computer system.
e. If Virginia wins a fellowship, she will go to graduate school.

EXERCISE T2-3 Verbs followed by gerunds or infinitives *page 53*

Possible sentences:
a. I enjoy riding my motorcycle.
b. Will you help Samantha study for the test?
c. The team hopes to work hard and win the championship.
d. Tom and his brothers miss surfing during the winter.
e. The babysitter let Roger stay up until midnight.

EXERCISE T3-1 Omissions and repetitions *page 53*

a. It is easy to learn how to operate our computers.
b. My grandfather is very old-fashioned.
c. The prime minister is the most popular leader in my country.
d. Pavel hasn't heard from the cousin whom he wrote to last month.
e. There are many skyscrapers in New York City.

EXERCISE T3-2 Order of cumulative adjectives *page 54*

a. an attractive young Vietnamese woman
b. a dedicated Catholic priest
c. her old blue wool sweater
d. Joe's delicious Scandinavian bread
e. many beautiful antique bird cages

EXERCISE T3-3 Present versus past participles *page 55*

a. My mother was annoyed at me for coming home late.
b. The noise in the hall was distracting to me.
c. Correct
d. The violence in recent movies is often disgusting.
e. Correct

PUNCTUATION

EXERCISE P1-1 The comma: independent clauses, introductory elements *page 56*

a. Correct
b. The man at the next table complained loudly, and the waiter stomped off in disgust.

c. Instead of eating half a cake or two dozen cookies, I now grab a banana or an orange.
d. Nursing is physically and mentally demanding, yet the pay is low.
e. After I won the hundred-yard dash, I found a bench in the park and collapsed.

EXERCISE P1-2   The comma: series, coordinate adjectives

a. She wore a black silk cape, a rhinestone collar, satin gloves, and high tops.
b. Correct
c. City Café is noted for its spicy vegetarian dishes and its friendly, efficient service.
d. Juan walked through the room with casual, elegant grace.
e. Correct

EXERCISE P1-3   The comma: nonrestrictive elements
page 58

a. We encountered no problems until we reached Cripple Creek, where the trail forked.
b. The Scott Pack, which is a twenty-five-pound steel bottle of air, is designed to be worn on a firefighter's back.
c. Correct
d. Shakespeare's tragedy *King Lear* was given a splendid performance by the actor Laurence Olivier.
e. Correct

EXERCISE P1-4   Major uses of the comma
page 59

a. The whiskey stills, which were run mostly by farmers and fishermen, were about twenty miles from the nearest town.
b. At the sound of a starting pistol, the horses surged forward toward the first obstacle, a sharp incline three feet high.
c. Each morning the seventy-year-old woman cleans the barn, shovels manure, and spreads clean hay around the milking stalls.
d. The students of Highpoint are required to wear dull green polyester pleated skirts.
e. You will be unable to answer all the clients' questions or solve all their problems, but you may turn to the directory when difficult issues arise.

EXERCISE P1-5   All uses of the comma
page 61

a. On January 29, 1990, we finally received Ms. Gilroy's reply to our letter of November 16, 1989.
b. The coach having bawled us out thoroughly, we left the locker room with his angry, harsh words ringing in our ears.
c. Good technique does not guarantee, however, that the power you develop will be sufficient for Kyok Pa competition.
d. We bought a home in Upper Marlboro, where my husband worked as a mail carrier.
e. Please make the check payable to David Kerr, D.D.S., not David Kerr, M.D.

Answers to Lettered Exercises   **99**

EXERCISE P2-1   Unnecessary commas   *page 62*

a. We'd rather spend our money on blue-chip stocks than speculate on porkbellies.
b. Being prepared for the worst is one way to escape disappointment.
c. When he heard the groans, he opened the door and ran out.
d. My father said that he would move to California if I would agree to transfer to UCLA.
e. I quickly accepted the fact that I was literally in third-class quarters.

EXERCISE P3-1   The semicolon and the comma   *page 64*

a. If fifty million people say a foolish thing, it is still a foolish thing.
b. No amount of experimentation can ever prove me right; a single experiment can prove me wrong.
c. Don't talk about yourself; it will be done when you leave.
d. The only sensible ends of literature are first, the pleasurable toil of writing; second, the gratification of one's family and friends; and lastly, the solid cash.
e. All animals are equal, but some animals are more equal than others.

EXERCISE P3-2   The semicolon and the comma   *page 65*

a. Correct
b. America has been called a country of pragmatists, although the American devotion to ideals is legendary.
c. The first requirement is honesty; everything else follows.
d. I am not fond of opera; I must admit, however, that I was greatly moved by *Les Misérables.*
e. Delegates to the convention came from Basel, Switzerland; Waikiki, Hawaii; Nome, Alaska; and Pretoria, South Africa.

EXERCISE P4-1   The colon, the semicolon, and the comma   *page 66*

a. The second and most memorable week of survival school consisted of five stages: orientation, long treks, POW camp, escape and evasion, and return to civilization.
b. Among the canceled classes were calculus, physics, advanced biology, and English 101.
c. His only desires were for vengeance: vengeance for his father's death, vengeance for his mother's loss of eyesight, vengeance for his own lost youth.
d. For example, when a student in a private school is caught with drugs, he or she is immediately expelled.
e. Correct

EXERCISE P5-1   The apostrophe   *page 68*

a. In a democracy anyone's vote counts as much as mine.
b. Correct
c. The puppy's favorite activity was chasing its tail.
d. After we bought J.J. the latest style pants and shirts, he decided that last year's faded, ragged jeans were perfect for all occasions.
e. A crocodile's life span is about thirteen years.

EXERCISE P6-1   Quotation marks page 69

a. "Fire and Ice" is one of Robert Frost's most famous poems.
b. As Emerson wrote in 1849, "I hate quotations. Tell me what you know."
c. Joggers have to run up the hills and then back down, but bicyclers, once they reach the top of a hill, get a free ride back down.
d. Correct
e. Historians Segal and Stineback tell us that the English settlers considered these epidemics "the hand of God making room for His followers in the 'New World.'"

EXERCISE P7-2   Other punctuation marks page 71

a. We lived in Davenport, Iowa, during the early years of our marriage.
b. Every night after her jazzercise class, Elizabeth bragged about how invigorated she felt, but she always looked exhausted.
c. Correct
d. Cancer — a disease that strikes without regard to age, race, or religion and causes dread in the most stalwart person — had struck my family. [or Cancer, . . . person, . . .]
e. The class stood, faced the flag, placed hands over hearts, and raced through "I pledge allegiance . . . liberty and justice for all" in less than sixty seconds.

MECHANICS

EXERCISE M1-1   Capital letters page 74

a. District Attorney Johnson was disgusted when the jurors turned in a verdict of not guilty after only one hour of deliberation.
b. My mother has begun to research the history of her Indian ancestors in North Carolina.
c. Correct
d. Refugees from Central America are finding it more and more difficult to cross the Rio Grande into the United States.
e. I want to take Environmental Biology 103, one other biology course, and one English course.

EXERCISE M2-1   Abbreviations page 75

a. Correct
b. My grandmother told me that of all the subjects she studied, she found economics the most challenging.
c. Correct
d. The first discovery of America was definitely not in A.D. 1492.
e. Turning to page 195, Marion realized that she had finally reached the end of chapter 22.

EXERCISE M3-1   Numbers page 76

a. We have ordered four azaleas, three rhododendrons, and two mountain laurels for the back area of the garden.
b. Correct
c. Correct

d. We ordered three 4-door sedans for company executives.
e. In 1989, only 102 male high school students in our state planned to make a career of teaching.

EXERCISE M4-1   Italics (underlining)   *page 77*

a. Howard Hughes commissioned the *Spruce Goose,* a beautifully built but thoroughly impractical wooden aircraft.
b. Pulaski was so exhausted he could barely lift his foot the six inches to the elevator floor.
c. Even though it is almost always hot in Mexico in the summer, you can usually find a cool spot on one of the park benches in the town's *zócalo.*
d. Correct
e. One of my favorite novels is George Eliot's *Middlemarch.*

EXERCISE M6-1   The hyphen   *page 80*

a. Correct
b. The quietly purring cat cleaned first one paw and then the other before curling up under the stove.
c. Many states are adopting laws that limit prop-
erty taxes for homeowners.
d. Your dog is well known in our neighborhood.
e. Correct

BASIC GRAMMAR

EXERCISE B1-1   Parts of speech: nouns   *page 81*

a. idea, words, freedom, movement; b. hands, devil's (noun/adjective), workshop; c. flower, concrete (noun/adjective), cloverleaf; d. censorship, flick, dial; e. Figures, liars

EXERCISE B1-2   Parts of speech: pronouns   *page 82*

a. Every (pronoun/adjective), its (pronoun/adjective), its (pronoun/adjective); b. those, who; c. I, some (pronoun/adjective), that, I, myself; d. who, his (pronoun/adjective); e. No one

EXERCISE B1-3   Parts of speech: verbs   *page 83*

a. have been; b. can be savored; c. does bring down; d. flock; e. Do scald

EXERCISE B1-4   Parts of speech: adjectives and adverbs   *page 84*

a. Adjectives: Little, great; b. Adjectives: The (article), American, tolerant; adverb: wonderfully; c. Adjectives: a (article), rotten; adverb: not; d. Adjectives: a (article), thin; adverb: very; e. Adjective: the (article); adverb: faster

EXERCISE B2-1　Parts of sentences: subjects

a. Complete subject: A spoiled child; simple subject: child; b. Complete subject: all facts; simple subject: facts; c. Complete subject: (You); d. Complete subject: nothing except change; simple subject: nothing; e. Complete subject: hope

EXERCISE B2-2　Parts of sentences: objects and complements

a. Direct object: a hundred fathers; subject complement: an orphan; b. Direct object: the depth of a river; c. Direct objects: your door, your neighbors; object complement: honest; d. Subject complement: a feast of lanterns; e. Indirect object: her father; direct object: forty whacks

EXERCISE B3-1　Subordinate word groups: prepositional phrases

a. with no side effects (adjective phrase modifying *tranquilizer*); b. on its back (adverbial phrase modifying *carries*); c. of money (adjective phrase modifying *love*), of all evil (adjective phrase modifying *root*); d. in a graveyard (adverbial phrase modifying *begins*), in a river (adverbial phrase modifying *ends*); e. with words (adverbial phrase modifying *can stroke*)

EXERCISE B3-2　Subordinate word groups: verbal phrases

a. being sixteen (gerund phrase used as subject complement); b. Concealing a disease (gerund phrase used as subject of the sentence), to cure it (infinitive phrase used as adjective modifying *way*); c. To help a friend (infinitive phrase used as subject of the sentence), to give ourselves pleasure (infinitive phrase used as subject complement); d. bearing gifts (participial phrase modifying *Greeks*); e. being dead (gerund phrase used as object of the preposition *by*)

EXERCISE B3-3　Subordinate word groups: subordinate clauses

a. Though you live near a forest (adverb clause modifying *do waste*); b. who help themselves (adjective clause modifying *those*); c. What is written without effort (noun clause used as subject of the sentence); d. that trots (adjective clause modifying *dog*); e. unless it is practiced on clever persons (adverb clause modifying *is practiced*)

EXERCISE B4-1　Sentence types

a. complex; who always speaks the truth (adjective clause); b. compound; c. simple; d. complex; If you don't go to other people's funerals (adverb clause); e. complex; who sleep like a baby (adjective clause)

Answers to Lettered Exercises　**103**